A *Simplified* GUIDE TO CONSTRUCTION LAW

BY JAMES ACRET

BNi Building News

BNI Building News

Editor-In-Chief
William D. Mahoney, P.E.

Design
Robert O. Wright
Eric F. Mahoney

BNI PUBLICATIONS, INC.

LOS ANGELES
10801 National Blvd.
Los Angeles, CA 90064

ANAHEIM
1612 S. Clementine St.
Anaheim CA 92802

BOSTON
629 Highland Ave.
Needham, MA 02194

WASHINGTON,D.C.
502 Maple Ave. West
Vienna, VA 22180

1-800-873-6397

ISBN 1-55701-176-1

Dedication

This book is dedicated by the author to his mother.

Acknowledgment

The author acknowledges the indispensable assistance of Laiah Lee.

CHAPTER 1

LAW

CHAPTER 1

LAW

1. Construction Law

The subject of "construction law" is extensive, and it can be made to seem complicated. But it can also be simplified. Part of a lawyer's everyday job is to make complicated things seem simple, but also to make simple things complicated. You'll understand what I mean if you go to the courthouse and listen to lawyers arguing about the law. One lawyer will be telling the judge that the issue is a simple one, easily decided. The opposing lawyer will likely be talking about the complexities of the case, and arguing the exceptions to a simple rule. There are those whose business it is to make the law seem complicated, but it is our business here to simplify a basic understanding of construction law.

The topic of construction law is extensive because the construction trade itself is extensive. The construction process has many diverse activities that invite the application of different fields of law. We will break down broad fields of law: contracts, torts, and real estate, for example, into parts that have a direct impact on the business of construction so as to make those parts understandable to the average contractor. Let us begin with a brief examination of what law is and how it works.

2. What Law Is

Law is to a democratic society and a free enterprise economy what the sea is to a fish: it is the very element from which democracy and business draw nourishment and life. This is no exaggeration. The collapse of communism is followed all around the world by recognition that democracy and enterprise depend upon the rule of law. Former communist nations struggling to enjoy the economic benefits of the industrial revolution, are finding that they are severely hampered by a lack of laws, judges, and, yes, even lawyers! Neither democracy nor business can exist without law and law enforcement. Without them, elections and contracts are meaningless.

3. Law

Law is rules of conduct. A law either requires, or prohibits, certain behavior. One law requires that a person obtain a license from the state before engaging in the contracting business, as another law prohibits false advertising by contractors. The very right to engage in the contracting business requires an understanding of law, because a licensed contractor must know what is required, and prohibited, by the contractors licensing law.

4. Statutes, Ordinances, and Regulations

Governmental power is divided between federal, state, and local government. Local government is divided between counties and cities. All governments exercise some of their power through commissions, districts, authorities, departments, and bureaus.

The United States congress and the legislatures of the 50 states pass laws known as "statutes". Cities and counties pass laws known as "ordinances". The various districts, boards, bureaus, authorities and agencies also have the power to pass laws, in this case known as "regulations". In case of conflict between federal and state, or local law, the U.S. Constitution provides that federal law is supreme. Likewise, state law controls law in the event of conflict with local law.

Examples of federal laws are OSHA (industrial safety), Davis Bacon (prevailing wage), and the Miller Act (requiring payment bonds on federal contracts). State and local laws that affect the construction industry include competitive bidding laws, contractors licensing laws, planning and zoning laws, building codes.

5. Interpretation of Statutes, Ordinances, and Regulations

Even the most carefully drafted laws are likely to be unclear in specific situations. It is the role of the courts to interpret the laws and to apply them to specific situations. If there is a question about whether a person has violated the contractors license law, or a parking regulation, or any other law, the question will be decided by a court.

The legislative power is separate from the judicial power and therefore the courts do not make laws, but only interpret them. The function of a court in interpreting a statute, ordinance, or regulation is to determine the intention of the agency that passed the law, whether the agency be the Congress of the United States, a state legislature, a city council, or a government agency.

6. Common Law

Statutes, ordinances, and regulations do not, and cannot, govern all human behavior or resolve all human disputes. Areas that are not covered by statutes, ordinances, or regulations are covered by the common law. Common law covers such topics as contracts, real estate, and torts: it is nothing more than the records of the decisions of judges in prior cases.

The colonists brought with them from England the common law, and after the revolution the states adopted it. (Louisiana, with a Spanish and French history, adopted the Code Napoleon.)

Common law had its beginnings in tradition. Legal scholars and reporters kept notes of court proceedings and reported how the judges decided cases. Other judges would consult these reports for guidance, and over the centuries there developed a rule called stare decisis. "Stare decisis" means "stand by things decided": so later judges follow the decisions of earlier judges.

Common law has proved marvelously adaptable to changing times. We now have such specialties as space law and electronics law. And courts are not immune to criticism, so occasionally they overrule earlier decisions. As one great judge said, "The life of the law has not been logic, it has been experience." (Oliver Wendell Holmes)

When people present a court with a question of contract law, the judge resolves the question by reviewing the records of decisions of courts in similar cases. The law to be applied by the judge in such a case is determined by examining the decisions that judges made in previous, similar cases. There is nothing mysterious or unusual about this kind of thinking. A pilot learns the stall characteristics of an airplane by looking it up in a book and the book is based on the experiences of other pilots in the same or similar airplanes. Questions of common law are resolved in much the same manner.

7. Appeal

Generally, the judicial system is divided into two branches: trial courts and appellate courts. A party who loses a lawsuit in the trial court always has the right to appeal the decision to a higher court. A Court of Appeal functions like the eraser on a pencil: it is there to correct mistakes. Between 20% and 30% of all trial court decisions are appealed to a higher court. Since a party is entitled to a trial that is free from error, a Court of Appeal will reverse the decision of a trial court if the decision is erroneous, and will order the trial court to correct the error or, if that is impossible, to retry the case.

8. Appellate Decisions

The decisions of the Courts of Appeal are made in writing, and the opinions are printed in law books. The law books are carefully indexed. Nowadays the opinions are not only in books, but in legal databases. Lawyers learn to look up rules of law in the opinions of the Courts of Appeal the way a student might look up a subject for a school paper in an encyclopedia.

9. Changing the Law

Both statutory law and the common law can always be changed by statute, and they often are. Judges also gradually change the common law so as to keep up-to-date with advances in technology, and changes in social and political thinking.

The common law is not abstract and theoretical. Every decision of every court is based on an actual dispute of some kind. The parties to a dispute present their cases and judges decide them. Thus, the development of common law depends on the self interest of the people in the lawsuit (litigants). Each party is entitled to be represented by a lawyer, and each lawyer's job is to find the cases supporting the interests of the client, and present those cases to the judge in a convincing way.

10. Advocacy

It sometimes seems as if lawyers and judges want to make the law seem complicated. To understand why this happens, you have to accept the fact that the

American legal system is based on advocacy. Justice can best be achieved if parties are free to advocate positions that advance their interests. Thus, runs the theory, each party will place before the judge all of the evidence and arguments that support his position, which will enable the judge to reach a fair result.

In the process of litigation, an advocate attempts to make strong points while confusing the strong points of the opponent. Lawyers don't like to admit ignorance, and ignorance of the law may be hidden behind a confusing cloud of jargon.

In this book, not every confusing exception to general rules will be discussed. The object here is to give a basic understanding of construction law that will help the reader to walk safely through the construction industry every day.

11. How Law is Made

Laws are made by the people (constitutions), by Congress and state legislatures (statutes), by cities and counties (ordinances), and, to a disturbing extent, by federal, state, and local agencies (regulations).

Bismarck said those who like treaties and sausages should not see how they are made. The same could be said of laws. It is sufficient for our purposes to understand that statutes are drafted and amended by Congress and the state legislatures with the assistance and advice, and under the influence of, lobbyists. Legislators are also politicians. Politicians are sometimes tempted to write ambiguous legislation so that they can interpret it as any particular audience of voters might want it to be interpreted.

12. Litigation

There are five phases of litigation: pleadings, discovery, motions, trial, and appeal.

Pleadings are formal legal statements of the positions of the parties: the claims of the plaintiff and the defenses of the defendant.

Discovery is a process that requires parties to answer questions, either orally (depositions) or in writing (interrogatories). The purpose of discovery is to permit parties to discover the truth, and assemble evidence that may be introduced at trial. Unfortunately, discovery may also be misused to intimidate and exhaust an opponent.

Motions, which are usually argued in open court, request that a judge make orders to make litigation easy or to decide issues in a case without trial.

The author assumes that readers know what a trial is like from observing the versions of them that are on television.

A Court of Appeal reviews portions of the record of the trial court (including pleadings and a transcript of the proceedings at the trial) brought to its attention by counsel, reads the briefs and listens to the arguments presented by counsel, and agrees with or reverses the decision of the trial court.

The loser of a case on appeal may petition the state Supreme Court for a hearing. A state Supreme Court will agree to review only a small percentage of the cases presented to it. The criteria for review are whether the case presents an important point of law, or an unsettled point of law that needs to be clarified, or a case in which the Court of Appeal made a wrong decision that needs to be reversed.

The federal court system has three branches: trial courts (district courts), circuit Courts of Appeal, and the United States Supreme Court. Most cases are handled by state courts. Federal courts have jurisdiction only to consider questions of federal law (statutes passed by the United States Congress), disputes between states, and cases that arise under the United States Constitution.

13. How ADR Fits In

Ambrose Bierce, in The Devil's Dictionary, defined *litigant: n. a person about to give up his skin for the hope of retaining his bones*. Bierce was alluding to the spiritual and monetary expense of litigation. The five phases of litigation are pleadings, discovery, motions, trial, and appeal. ADR (alternative dispute resolution) may remove three, four, or even all five phases.

The most popular form of ADR is arbitration, which is provided for in a majority of construction contracts and subcontracts. Arbitration completely removes phases 2 and 5 (discovery and appeal) and effectively removes phases 1 and 3 (pleadings and motions).

The next most popular form of ADR, mediation, removes all five phases of litigation.

14. Arbitration

Arbitration is a system under which the parties to a dispute appoint an arbitrator whose decision is as enforceable as the decision of a judge and not subject to appeal. Unless otherwise agreed, there is no discovery. *Motions* are usually minimal, or non-existent in arbitration. *Pleadings* in arbitration are a simple statement of a demand for relief by the claimant, and an answering statement (which is optional) by the responding party.

15. Mediation

Mediation differs from arbitration in that a mediator has no power to make an enforceable decision. The function of a mediator is to help the parties resolve their own dispute. Experience shows that when parties have a sincere desire to resolve a dispute, mediation is successful in more than 90% of the cases.

Case in Point

The Arizona Supreme Court held that an arbitration agreement that was "grossly inequitable" was not enforceable by a property owner against a construction contractor. An addendum to a construction contract provided that the owner had the option of either selecting arbitration or litigation in court as the means for resolving any dispute, and the addendum also gave the owner the right to change his mind at any time up to final judgment. The court held that an arbitration agreement has to be enforceable by both sides in order for it to be enforceable by either side. The court said that the agreement was so grossly inequitable that it ran counter to the philosophy of encouraging arbitration and that, under the circumstances, the arbitration agreement was unenforceable and the parties would be required to resolve their dispute by litigation in court. Stevens/ Leinweber/ Sullens, Inc v Holm Development & Management, Inc, 165 Ariz 25 (1990).

CHAPTER 2

FORMATION AND INTERPRETATION OF CONTRACTS

CHAPTER 2

FORMATION AND INTERPRETATION OF CONTRACTS

1. Exchange

The purpose of the construction industry is to exchange services, equipment, and materials for money. The terms of the exchange are governed by contracts. Architects, engineers, construction managers, prime contractors, subcontractors, and equipment and material suppliers all work with agreements, contracts, subcontracts, and purchase orders, most of which are written in standard forms. Others are specially written for the occasion.

2. Special Requirements

Many states have special rules for certain types of construction contracts. Some states, for example, require that home remodeling contracts must be in writing and clearly specify the construction schedule, the payment schedule, and the equipment and materials for the job. Some states require that a homeowner be given a three day "cooling off period" to cancel certain types of home improvement contracts. Some states require that construction contracts include notices that warn consumers about the potential hazards of mechanics lien claims.

3. Construction Contracts: The Big Picture

The principle that people are free to contract for any lawful purpose is an important feature of our economy. In order for the market to work, it is essential that a nation have laws that make contracts enforceable and establish a court system with the power to enforce them. The importance of these legal institutions has become obvious in the 1990's, as nations attempt to convert from communism to market economies.

American law grants freedom of contract. The terms that may be found in construction industry contracts are as different and clever as good businessmen can make them.

4. Entering into a Contract -- Mutual Assent

K: "I will prune your trees for $150."

O: "Deal."

This is a legally enforceable contract. It is an exchange of promises. Each party has voluntarily promised to do something in exchange for a promise by the other party to do something. If the parties should fall into dispute about the number of limbs to be removed, the law will give that element a reasonable interpretation. In making such an interpretation, the court would consider evidence of trade practice.

5. Signature

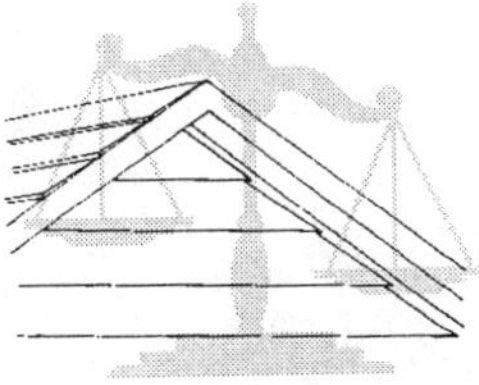

K sends two copies of her standard subcontract form to S, who signs and returns both copies to K. K signs both copies, but then has second thoughts about S. K decides to think things over, puts both copies in the file, and finally decides to award the contract to S-2.

No contract. The acceptance of an offer is not effective until it is spoken to or sent to the person making the offer.

6. Failure to Read

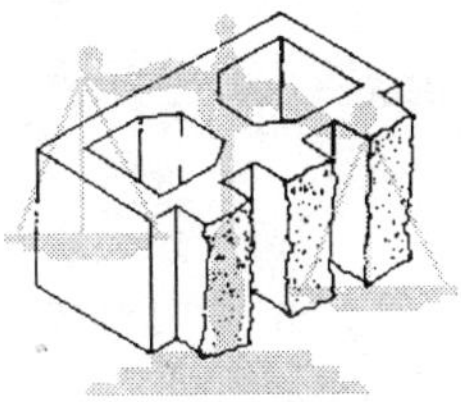

K sends O a form contract for construction of an apartment building. O, without reading the contract, signs it and returns it to K. After K commences work, O cancels the contract.

O committed a breach of contract. Failure to read a contract does not prevent the formation of a contract.

7. Acceptance by Conduct

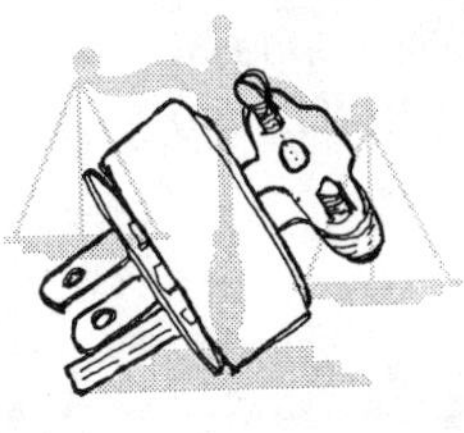

S is standing on a street corner with bags of oranges and a sign that says "$1.00". B rolls down the window of his car and takes a bag.

This conduct creates a contract. B owes S $1.00. Although no words have been spoken, S has indicated an intention to sell the bag of oranges, and B has indicated a promise to pay for them.

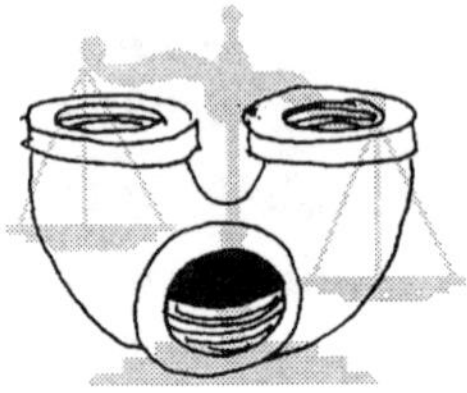

K sends S two copies of an unsigned subcontract form. S makes a copy for himself, signs two copies and sends them back to K. K puts the forms aside and doesn't sign them. K schedules S into the job, and S starts work. S's first request for payment does not comply with the requirements of the contract form so K returns it and demands that S revise the request for payment per contract. S complies, and K makes the first payment.

Contract! Although K didn't sign the contract, she followed its provisions and demanded that S also do so. This is sufficient acceptance to form a contract.

8. Unilateral Contract

Legalese. *Lawyers sometimes distinguish between bilateral contracts and unilateral contracts. A bilateral contract is an exchange of promises. A unilateral contract is an offer that can only be accepted by performance of an act.*

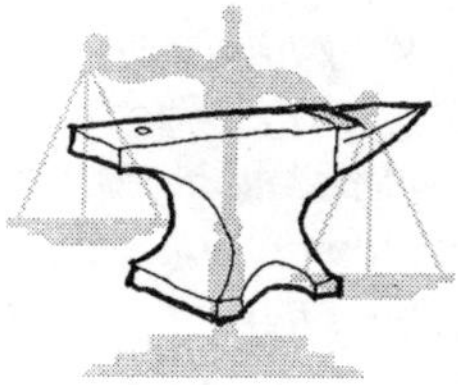

O: "I'll pay you $5 to mow my lawn."
G: "I accept."

This is a two-way (bilateral) contract because the parties have exchanged promises.

O: "If you mow my lawn I will pay you $5."

G: [Mows lawn].

This is a one-way (unilateral) contract. The only way G could accept O's offer was by mowing the lawn, rather than by promising to mow the lawn.

9. Sort of a Contract

K and S trade forms, but S never accepts K's form and she never accepts his. Nevertheless K schedules S onto the job, S starts work, and K makes progress payments.

Sort of a contract! (Lawyers call this a quasi contract.) There is no contract because neither party ever accepted the other party's offer. The law treats this as a contract for S to perform work according to trade practice and for K to pay the reasonable value of the work.

Legalese. *(Note: Read this part only if you are a lawyer or want to be able to talk like one.) The formation of a contract requires a manifestation of mutual assent. This is usually accomplished either by signing a document or by offer and acceptance. When parties express their consent without using words (as taking a bag of oranges from a street vendor) we have a contract in fact. The doctrine of contract in law or quasi contract, comes into play in cases where there is no manifestation of mutual assent and therefore no contract, but a contract is implied in law to prevent the unjust enrichment of one party at the expense of another. The doctrine only applies in cases where there is no expression by one party of any intention to make a gift to the other party.*

10. Counter-Offer

K: "I'll prune your trees for $150." O: "I'll give you $125." K: [Says nothing]. O: "All right, I'll give you $150."

No contract. O's rejection killed the offer.

11. Withdrawal of Offer

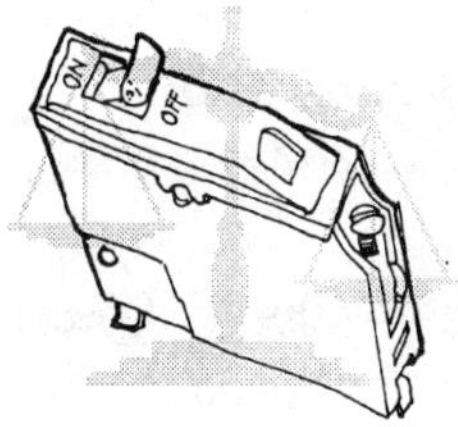

Monday. K: "I will build your warehouse per plans and specs for $500,000. This offer will remain open for 48 hours."

Tuesday. O: Posts a letter accepting the offer.

Tuesday. K: Sends a fax withdrawing the offer.

No contract. An unaccepted offer can be withdrawn at any time. Acceptance of an offer is not effective until it is received.

12. Option

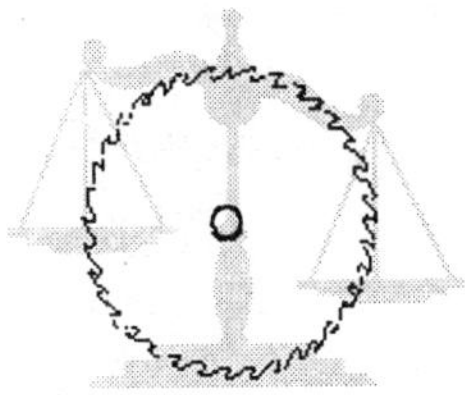

Same as above, except O paid K $10 to keep the offer open for two days.

Contract. The promise to keep the offer open for 48 hours was supported by consideration (the $10). This kind of an offer is known as an "option". An option gives the person getting the offer (offeree) the right, for a specified period of time, to either accept or reject the offer. An option itself is a contract, and the withdrawal of an option is a breach of contract.

13. Bid Withdrawn

K submits a sealed written bid to build a private hospital for $7.5 million. Ten minutes before bid opening time, K notifies the hospital that the bid is withdrawn. When bids are opened, K's bid is low, and the hospital accepts it.

No contract. K had the legal right to withdraw the bid at any time before it was accepted.

14. Letter of Intent

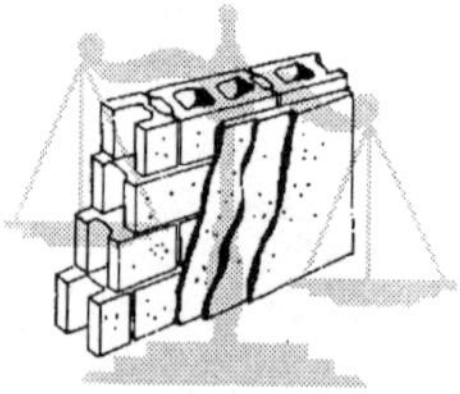

O sends K a letter confirming that it intends to award a contract to K for the construction of an apartment complex. After a change of heart, O awards the contract to K-2.

No contract. O did not enter into a contract with K, but indicated an intention to enter into such a contract. A letter of intent does not usually rise to the level of a contract.

15. Duress

K threatens to break O's leg unless O signs a contract. O signs. O refuses to perform the contract.

A contract signed under threat or intimidation (duress) is unenforceable.

16. Economic Duress

O, who owes K $120,000, knowing that K can't meet payroll, offers to pay $50,000 in exchange for a full release. K signs the release and takes the $50,000, then claims the balance.

Under some circumstances, although rarely, the law recognizes that economic intimidation invalidates a release.

17. Promissory Estoppel

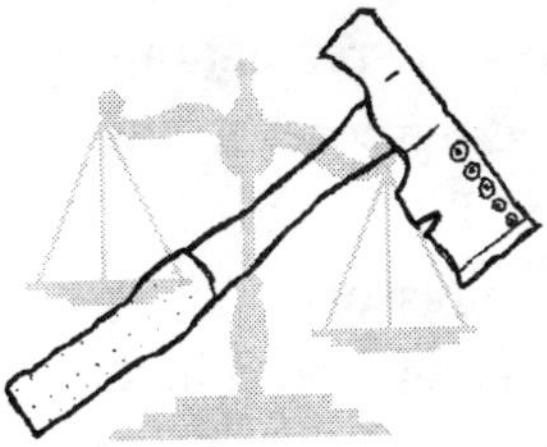

K, who is bidding a hospital job, receives a $400,000 telephone bid from S for plumbing per plans and specs. K uses S's bid in compiling its own bid. The hospital awards the job to K. S, discovering a mistake in its estimate, then withdraws its bid.

S does not have the legal right to withdraw its bid. This is because K relied on S's bid in preparing his own bid. This is known as the doctrine of promissory estoppel. "Estoppel" means "prevented from changing position"

18. Damages

K awards the plumbing subcontract to the next low bidder for $440,000.

K will recover judgment from S for $40,000: the difference between the bid and the cost of the plumbing contract.

19. The Uniform Commercial Code

In medieval times merchants throughout Europe began to agree to a set of rules and regulations governing international commerce. The purpose of this law merchant was to make trade easier. Early trade law merchant treats such subjects as promissory notes, drafts, checks, letters of credit, warehouse receipts, bills of lading, and sales. An important objective of law merchant is uniform application and interpretation throughout the world.

In the United States law merchant evolved into the Uniform Commercial Code (UCC) which has been adopted in all states. The UCC has its own version of the doctrine of promissory estoppel which is watered down from the version that applies under the law of contracts.

The doctrine of promissory estoppel applies to subcontractor bids, but the UCC governs bids submitted by manufacturers and material suppliers.

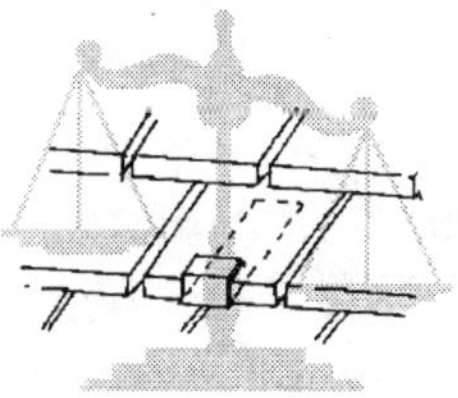

S (supplier) submits a bid to K (prime contractor) for switchgear to be used by K in the construction of a powerhouse owned by a public agency. The bid is for $700,000. The next low bid for the same switchgear is $900,000. K uses the $700,000 bid submitted by S in figuring its bid for the prime contract. The job is awarded to K. S then retracts the bid over K's protest. K purchases the switchgear from S's competitor for $900,000 and makes a claim against S for the difference of $200,000.

Under the doctrine of promissory estoppel, K would have a good claim against S, but the Uniform Commercial Code applies rather than the law of contracts because the relationship between K and S was that of buyer and seller rather than that of contractor and subcontractor.

Under the UCC, a material supplier's bid to a contractor that is relied upon by the contractor in submitting its bid for a construction contract is can’t be withdrawn for ten days after the award of the contract, but if a bid is oral and exceeds $2,500 the irrevocability does not apply unless the contractor confirms the bid in writing within 48 hours.

20. Public Bidding

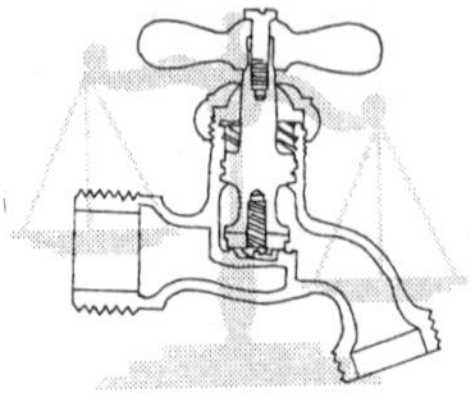

K, a licensed contractor, submits a low bid of $7,500,000 to construct a public hospital. The hospital awards the job to the second low bidder for $7,520,000.

The award to the second low bidder is illegal. Competitive bidding statutes require public agencies to award contracts to the lowest responsible bidder. In some states, K would recover from the hospital authority its anticipated profit. In other states, K could recover only its costs of preparing the bid.

21. Private Competitive Bidding

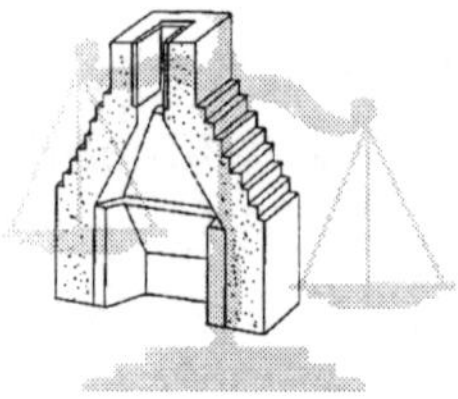

H, a private hospital, decides to award a contract to the second low bidder for $7,520,000 rather than to the low bidder, whose figure was $7,500,000.

As a private party, H is legally entitled to reject any and all bids.

22. Auction

B bids $75 for a grand piano at an auction. The auctioneer withdraws the grand piano and refuses to sell it at that price.

The bid was an offer, and the auctioneer had the right to reject the offer.

23. Auction without Reserve

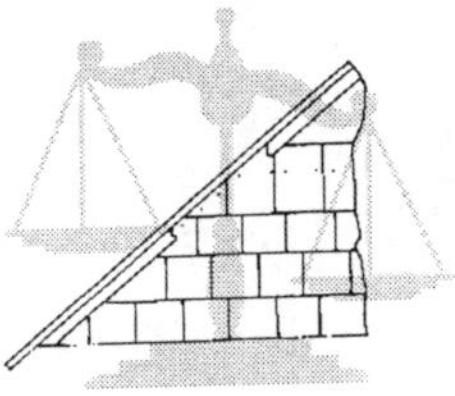

Same as above, but the auctioneer had announced in advance that the auction was without reserve.

Here, the auctioneer is legally obliged to accept the high bid.

24. No Consideration

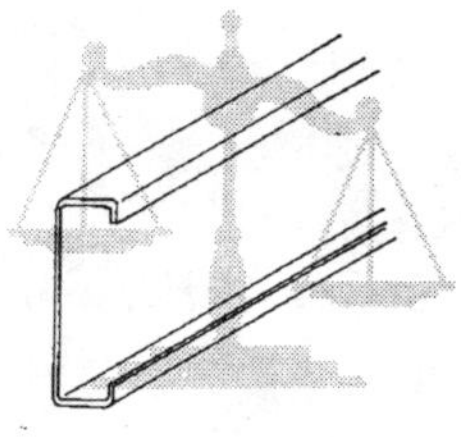

Grandpa: "I'm going to take you to Disneyland next Saturday." Kids: "Hey, thanks Grandpa."

No contract. Although Grandpa's offer was accepted, it wasn't supported by consideration.

25. Consideration

Grandpa calls a limo to take the kids to Disneyland.

Contract between Grandpa and the limo company. Consideration on one side (driving to Disneyland) is supported by consideration on the other side (payment).

26. Adequacy of Consideration

I will give you my new Chevy if you will push a peanut from Main Street to Broadway with your nose.

Contract. The law does not concern itself with the amount of consideration.

27. Illegal Consideration

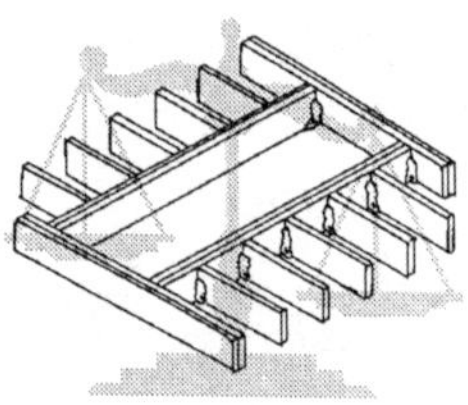

I'll pay you $100 to deliver a package of marijuana.

No contract. The consideration (delivery of drugs) is illegal.

28. Clerical Mistake

K receives ten bids for the mechanical work on a hospital job. The high bid is $1.2 million, the low bid is $600,000, the next low bid is $1.1 million. K accepts the low bid and signs a contract with S. S then reviews its estimate and discovers that, because of a misplaced decimal point, his bid was $700,000 lower than intended. S refuses to perform.

No contract. S's bid was the product of clerical mistake and K, because of the distribution of the other nine bids, either knew, or should have known, that the bid was a mistake.

29. Mistake of Judgment

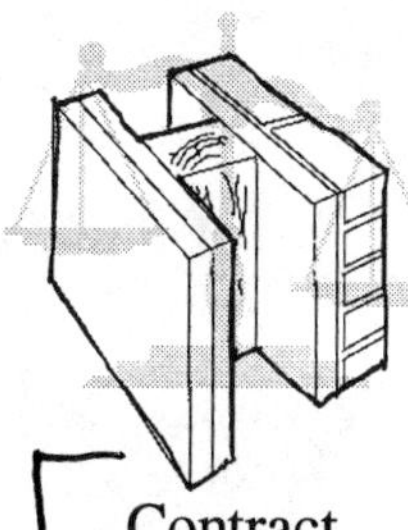

Same as above, except that S's mistake was that he thought he could convince the hospital to accept substitution of an equal, but less expensive, mechanical system.

Contract. A mistake in judgment doesn't prevent formation of a contract.

30. Illusory Consideration

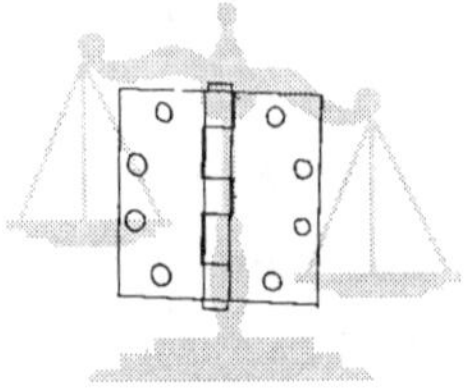

O and K sign a contract for construction of a $12.5 million hospital. O reserves the right to cancel the contract at any time for any reason, or no reason. Before work commences, K cancels the contract.

No contract. The consideration was illusory since O could decide not to perform.

31. Failure of Consideration

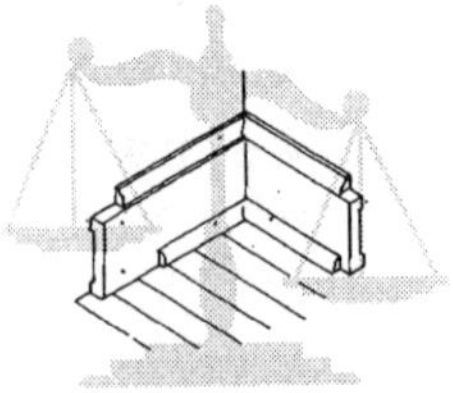

B: "I will buy your horse for $100: $25 down and $75 upon delivery."

S: "Done!"

A contract has been formed.

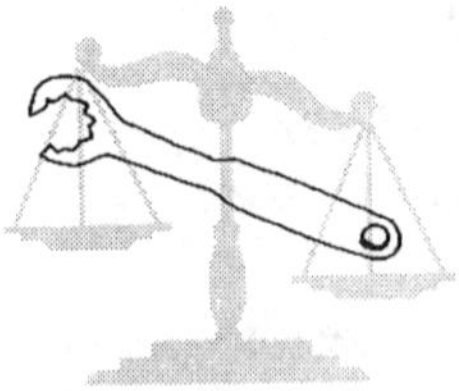

. . . B pays the $25. Then, before delivery, the horse dies.

B is excused by failure of consideration from the duty to pay the balance of the purchase price.

Same as above, but B agrees to make the $25 down payment on June 1. June 1 arrives, and B fails to make the payment.

B has committed a breach of contract. S can recover judgment for $25.

32. Failure of Consideration after Breach of Contract

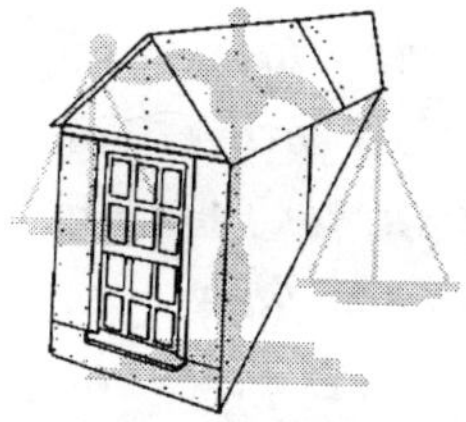

Same as above, but the horse dies on June 2.

B is excused from performance by failure of consideration. The failure of consideration "cured" the $25 breach.

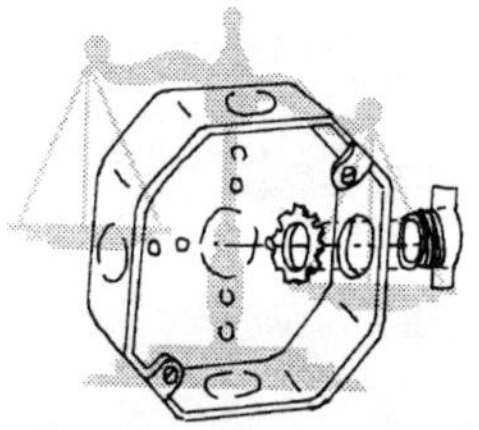

K signs a contract to build a hospital for O for $7,500,000. A mobilization payment is due on June 1. O fails to make the payment. On June 2, K's contractors license is revoked.

O breached the contract by failing to make the $100,000 mobilization payment, but the breach is excused by failure of consideration since K cannot legally perform any construction work.

33. Incompetence

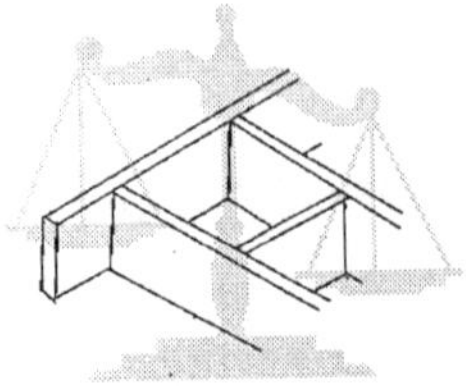

K, 15 years old, signs a contract to prune O's trees for $500. O cancels the contract.

There was no enforceable contract. A minor is not old enough to contract.

34. Interpretation of Contract - Trade Practice

S signs a contract to install sewers on a subdivision project for developer D. The contract requires S to start work within ten days after written notice from D. D gives the written notice but S refuses to start. S proves that trade practice is for the sewer contractor to start work only after the developer has rough graded the streets.

Trade practice prevails. There is an implied promise

35. Typewriting versus Printing

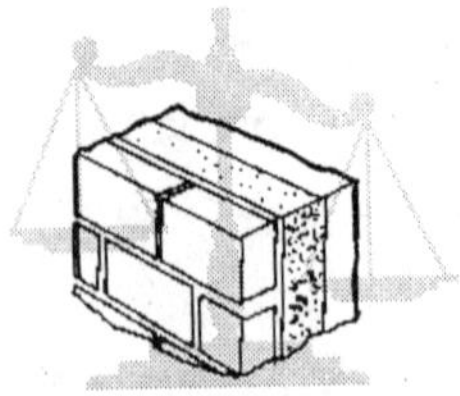

Form contract provides that the owner will withhold a 10% retention. Typewritten portion of the contract provides for 5% retention.

Typewritten provisions control printed provisions.

The presumption is that the parties gave special attention to the typewritten provisions.

36. Ambiguity Caused by the Drafter

Ambiguity (uncertainty) caused by the drafter of a contract is interpreted against the drafter.

37. Conflict between Plans and Specifications

The plans for an air conditioning system call for 50 cfm and the specifications require 100 cfm. Subcontractor figured the job from the plans and supplies 50 cfm

Ambiguity will be construed against the drafter.

Same facts, but the general conditions of the contract provide that in case of conflict the more stringent requirement prevails.

This provision controls the general rule that ambiguities are interpreted (construed) against the drafter.

38. Satisfaction Clause

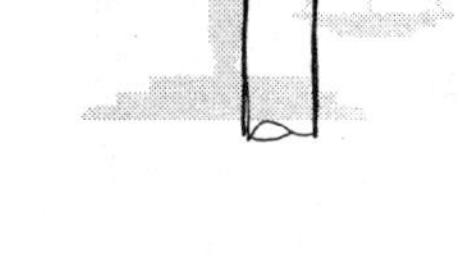

Contract provides that contractor's work will meet the satisfaction of the owner. Although the contractor's performance appears to be first class, owner is "dissatisfied".

"Satisfaction clauses" are interpreted to require only that degree of performance that would satisfy a reasonable person.

Case in Point

A federal Court of Appeals held that demands for a perfectly uniform finish on aluminum walls in a Chevrolet plant were not enforceable even though the contract provided that final acceptability would rest strictly with the owner. A subcontractor had installed aluminum walls that, in bright sunlight, did not appear to have a uniform finish and therefore the owner rejected the work. The walls were replaced by another subcontractor, and, as replaced, were accepted. The court said that when a contract deals with commercial and mechanical utility, and calls for the contractor to achieve the personal satisfaction of the owner, courts will only hold the contractor to a standard of work that would be satisfactory to a reasonable person. In this case the type of wall specified was a mill finish. It was shown to be difficult, practically impossible, to achieve a perfectly uniform finish with such a type of aluminum. Morin Building Products Co v Baystone Construction, Inc, 717 Fed 2d 413 (7th Cir 1983).

CHAPTER 3

CHANGES AND EXTRAS

CHAPTER 3

CHANGES AND EXTRAS

1. Changes

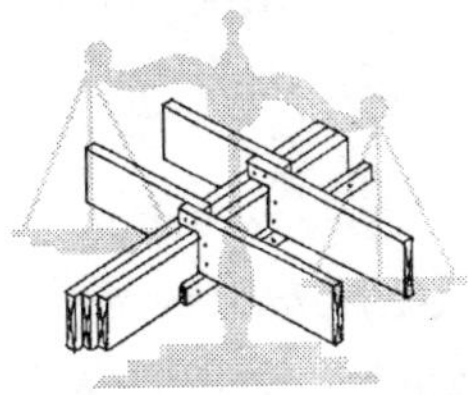

O and K, parties to a written contract for construction of a hospital, sign a change order increasing air handling capacity of a unit from 50 to 100 cfm. The contract price is increased accordingly.

A written contract can be modified by a written contract. Here, the change is supported by consideration on both sides and the contract will be enforced as modified.

2. Consideration for Modification

Under a contract, B is required to make payments to S of $100 a month for ten months. S tells B he can skip the tenth payment, then sues for it.

Here, the contract was not modified because the attempted modification was not supported by consideration on both sides. S gave up $10, but B didn't give up anything.

3. Oral Modification of Written Contract

O and K, parties to a written construction contract, orally agree that K will double-glaze windows for an additional $5,000. K refuses to perform.

No breach. A written contract may not be modified by an unperformed oral agreement.

O and K, parties to a written construction contract, orally agree that K will double-glaze windows for an additional $5,000. K performs, but O refuses to pay the extra.

O breached the contract. An oral modification is enforceable after it has been fully performed on one side.

Legalese. *In legalese, a contract that has been "executed" is a contract that has been "performed". Another legal meaning for "executed" is "signed".*

Same as above, but the contract provides that it may not be modified except by a written change order signed by both parties.

The modification holds. A party may waive provisions inserted into a contract for its benefit. A provision requiring that change orders be in writing was put in the contract for the benefit of O, and O therefore could waive the requirement.

4. Estoppel

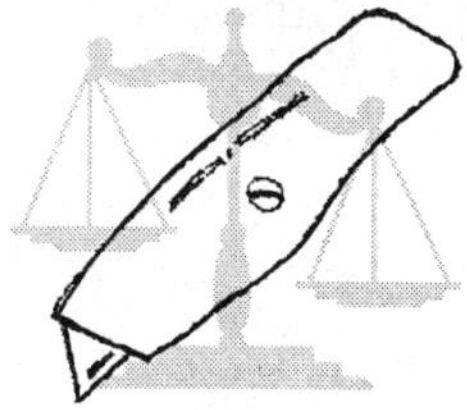

O: "I want you to buy double-glazed windows." K: "I don't have any money." O: "I already put $5,000 in your account." K: [Buys windows].

No contract. O did not make a promise, but a statement of fact. But under the doctrine of estoppel, the law will force O to stand by the statement of fact.

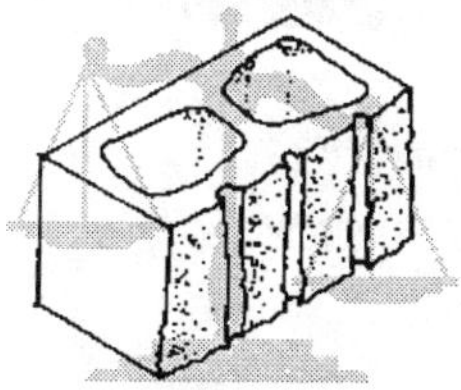

Same as above, but K and O have signed a contract that provides for no extra compensation without a written change order.

The estoppel still holds, and O will be required to put the $5,000 in K's account.

5. Waiver of Contract Requirements

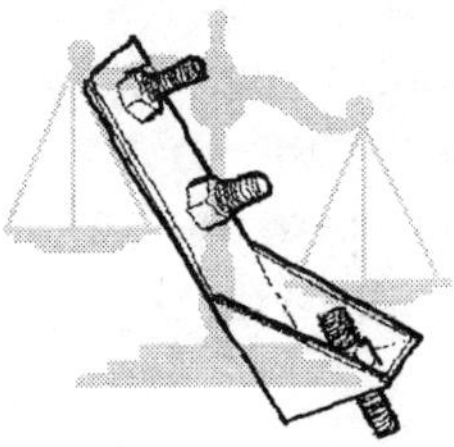

O: "Double-glaze the windows and I'll pay whatever it costs." K: "But the contract requires that change orders be in writing." O: "Don't bother with that. Trust me. I'll pay for it." K: [Performs, and bills O

for the extra work]. O: "I'm not going to pay you because you didn't get a written change order."

O must pay. She waived the written change order requirement. A party may waive provisions that were put into a contract for her benefit.

6. Refusal to Change

Contract provides that no changes will be made without a written change order specifying the price of the change and signed by both parties.

O issues a change order in writing, requiring K to double-glaze windows for $5,000 (a reasonable price.) K refuses to sign the change order, holding out for a price of $10,000.

Here, K has a contractual right to perform the contract according to its terms and single-glaze the windows. O can't change the contract terms without K's consent.

Business Pointer

For her own protection, O should retain the right to issue change orders. Absent agreement on the price for a change, the contract may provide for payment to the contractor on a cost plus basis.

Case in Point

A contractor cannot recover extra compensation for dealing with underground conditions when the contract document places the risk of unforeseen difficulties squarely on the contractor. A federal Court of Appeals considered a case in which a contractor sued a utility for extra compensation because of cost overruns in the construction of an earthen dam. Bidders were provided with a geotechnical report but were instructed to make their own investigations since no price adjustment would be made for unforeseen underground conditions. The clay soil at the site of the dam contained more moisture than was indicated in the geotechnical report and the dam developed cracks. Contractor claimed extra compensation for the cost of dealing with the wet clay. The court held that a contractor who agrees to build a job for a fixed cost must absorb any losses resulting from unforeseen conditions where the risk of such losses is placed on the contractor. Green Construction Co v Kansas Power and Light Co, 1 Fed 3d 1005 (10th Cir 1993).

CHAPTER 4

BREACH OF CONTRACT

18. Penalty Clauses

19. Bonus Clauses

20. Contractor's Damages for Delay

21. Foreseeable Damages

CHAPTER 4

BREACH OF CONTRACT

1. Breach of Contract

Suppose that K (contractor) and O (owner) sign a contract for construction of a concrete driveway. K then gets an opportunity to bid a profitable job elsewhere, leaves town, and fails to perform. What are O's legal rights?

In this sample case, K has breached the contract. O, having been injured by the breach of contract, is entitled to collect compensation from K. The amount of compensation is the amount that will put O in the same economic position it would have been in if K had performed.

2. Substantial Performance

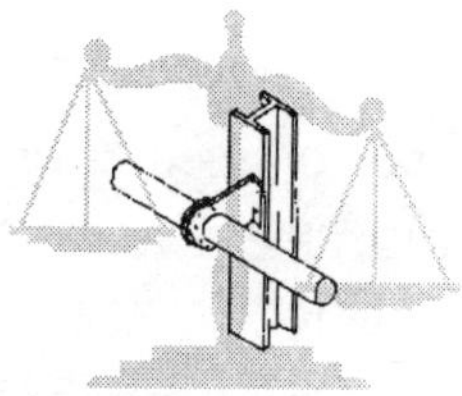

The specifications for a plumbing system of an apartment complex call for steel pipe. Contractor misreads the specifications and installs copper pipe. Owner refuses to pay the contract price, alleging breach of contract.

The contractor would be entitled to recover the

contract price. The contractor acted in good faith, and the end product is no less valuable than it would have been if the steel pipe had been installed.

3. Substantial Performance Inferior

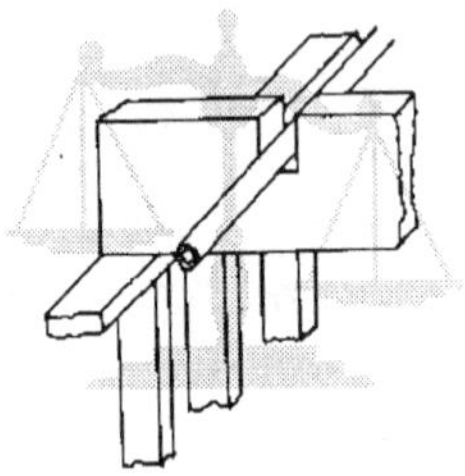

Same as above, except contractor mistakenly installed steel pipe rather than copper pipe.

Here, the contractor would be entitled to recover the contract price less the reduction in value of the apartment complex resulting from the substitution of steel or copper pipe. The contract was substantially performed.

4. Willful Failure

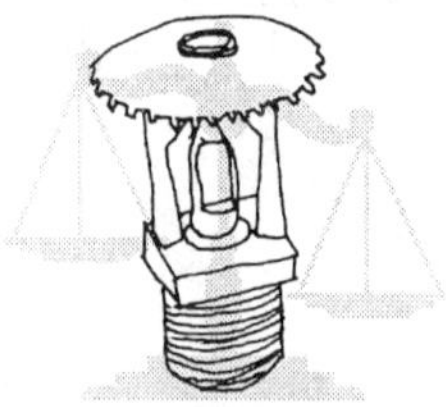

Contractor intentionally installed steel pipe rather than copper pipe as specified in order to save money, and tries to conceal the substitution from the owner.

Here, the contractor would not be entitled to recover damages for breach of contract from the owner, because the contractor failed to substantially perform the contract. The doctrine of substantial performance does not aid a person who commits an intentional, willful breach of contract.

5. Punitive Damages

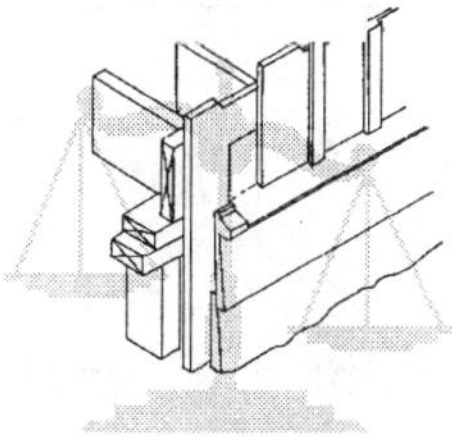

K refuses to perform a written contract for construction of an apartment complex because she has an opportunity to perform a more profitable job in another city. O sues for breach of contract and seeks to recover punitive damages for the willful breach.

Punitive damages are not available for breach of contract, even if the breach is willful.

6. Damages for Breach of Contract

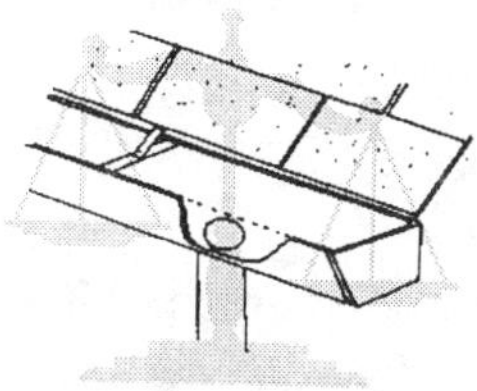

Assume that the contract price between K and O was $2,000. Discovering that K has left town, O employs K-2 to build the driveway for $1,850.

In this case, O has not been damaged by the breach of contract because O has saved $150 by signing with K-2. Therefore O has no legal right to collect damages from K.

7. Compensatory Damages

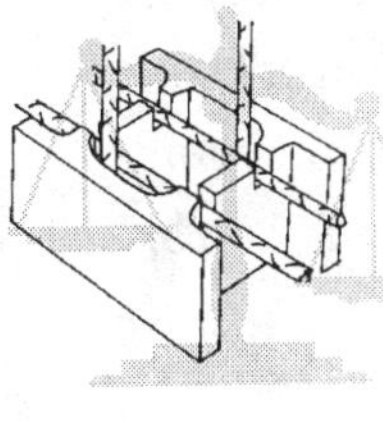

Now suppose that O, after taking three bids, signs a contract with K-2, the low bidder, to build the driveway for $2,500.

Here, O would take judgment against K for $500. $500 is the amount that would make up for the loss. O had apparently made a good bargain with K, and under the law O is entitled to the benefit of the bargain.

The damages that the law awards for breach of contract are not awarded for the purpose of punishing K, but merely to protect the contract by compensating O for the economic loss caused by the breach.

8. Breach by Owner

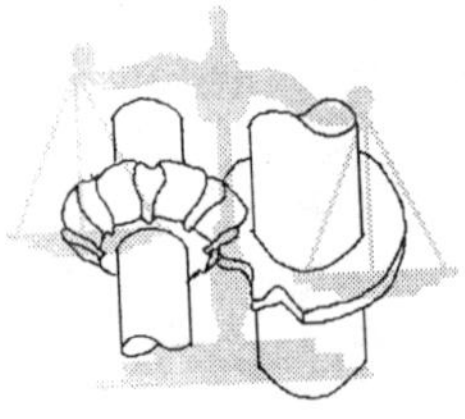

Now suppose that K signs a contract to build a warehouse for O. The contract price is $700,000. O then gets an opportunity to rent a warehouse at a good price, and decides to cancel the contract with K.

Here, O has breached the contract and therefore K is entitled to recover damages from O. How are the damages calculated?

9. Loss of Profit

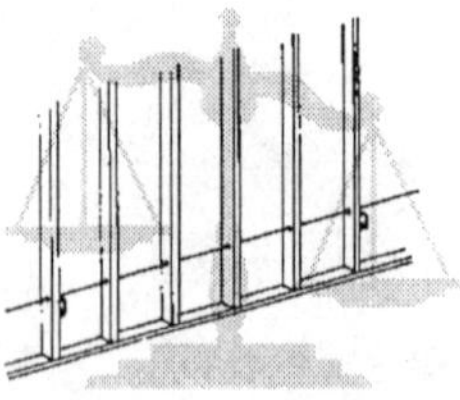

K reviews her estimate. She figured the cost of all labor, material, subcontracts, taxes, fringes, and jobsite overhead and then added 9½% for home office overhead and 7% for profit.

K may recover the profit, but not the overhead. By awarding her the profit, the law puts K in the same economic position she would have enjoyed if O had performed the contract.

10. Interest

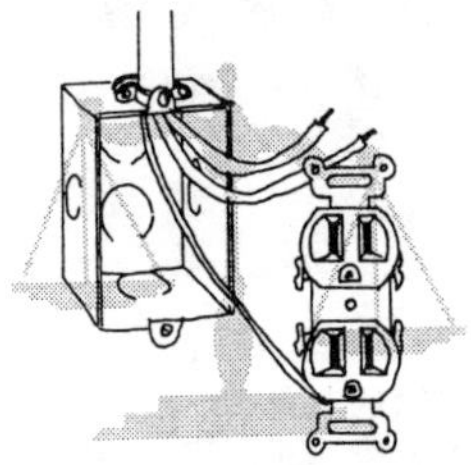

It takes three years for K process her claim through the courts. She proves that if she had performed the contract she would have received full payment by June 1, 1997.

Here, part of the damage that K has suffered because of O's breach is loss of the interest that she could have earned on the profit if O had performed his side of the contract. An award of interest would compensate her for this loss.

11. Attorneys Fees

K points out to the judge that the profit plus interest, altogether, is less than $100,000, which leaves her a net of only $30,000 after paying attorneys fees and litigation expenses. Her contract, however, does not have an attorneys fees clause in it.

K is not entitled to recover attorneys fees. Under the American rule, attorneys fees are awarded for breach of contract only if the contract so provides.

Business Pointer

When drafting a construction contract, one of the important points to be decided is whether to include an attorneys fees clause. Lawsuits, of course, are never wanted or expected when a construction contract is signed. But this does not mean that the parties should not plan for a lawsuit if it should occur.

In the last analysis, since attorneys fees are awarded to the winning party, a contractor will want to include an attorneys fees clause if he expects that he is likely to be the winner. If the contractor expects that in the event of a lawsuit he is likely to be the loser, he will not want to include an attorneys fees clause in the contract. There are so many uncertainties in the construction process that general contractors should usually avoid attorneys fees clauses in their prime contracts. One reason is that a general contractor is responsible to the owner for all the failures of its subcontractors and suppliers.

General contractors may also be reluctant to include attorneys fees clauses in their subcontracts because, in effect, the general contractor may be legally responsible to subcontractors for problems that are really caused by the owner or the architect.

With similar thinking, owners, subcontractors, and suppliers usually favor the inclusion of attorneys fees clauses.

12. Stopping the Work

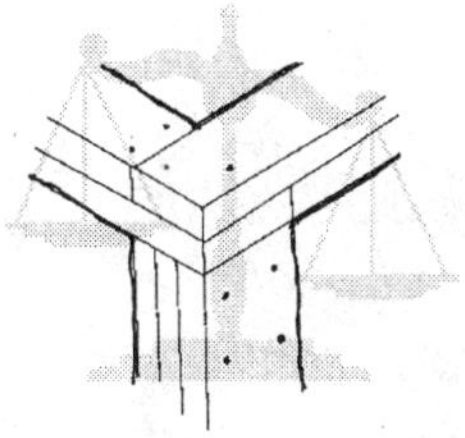

After performing work for one month, K submits a request for payment as provided by the contract. O fails to make payment within ten days as the contract requires. K continues to work for another ten days, then stops work. O complains that K has breached the contract.

Here, K had the right to stop work. K's further performance is excused by O's breach.

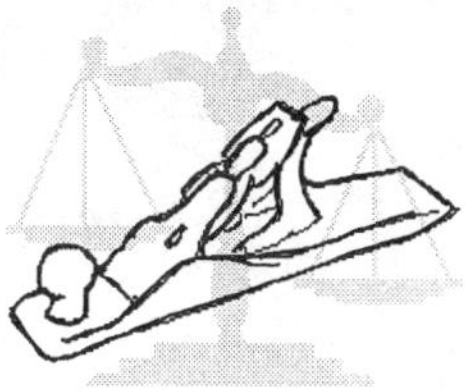

O refuses to make a progress payment to K because K failed to attain 90% compaction of fill. K stops work.

Here, O's obligation to make the progress payment was excused by K's prior breach. Stopping work in such a case is another breach of contract by K.

Same facts as above, O orders K to leave the job and employs another contractor to correct the defective grading and proceed with the work.

Here, O's action is justified by K's breach of contract.

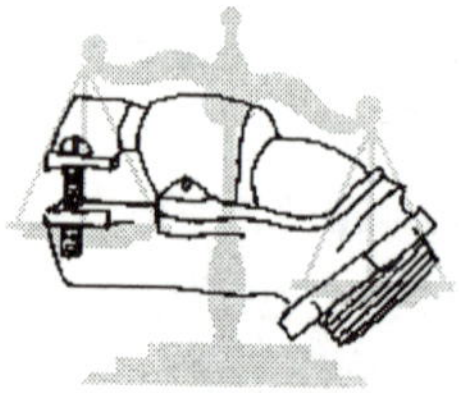

Contract requires O to make progress payments by the 10th of the month. On the 12th of the month, K, not having received payment, demobilizes and abandons the work.

Here, K was not justified in abandoning the work because O's breach was not material.

A material breach is defined as a substantial one, a breach that deprives a party of the important benefits of a contract. Absent unusual circumstances, a delay of two days in making payment would not be considered a material breach of contract.

13. Anticipatory Breach

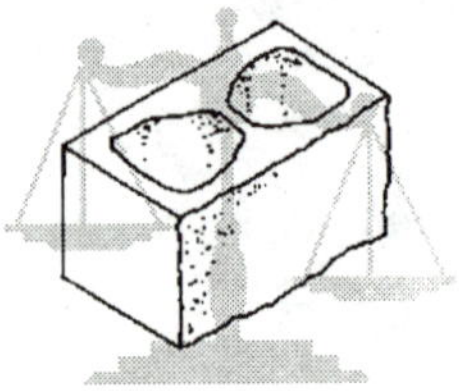

K has earned a progress payment of $65,000 payable June 10. On June 1, K submits a request for payment for $120,000. K informs O that he will stop work and abandon the job unless O pays $120,000 no later than June 10. Meanwhile K continues to man the job.

Here, K has not actually breached the contract but has said in a positive manner that he is going to breach the contract. This statement, in itself, is a breach of contract.

__Legalese.__ An unequivocal statement that one intends to breach a contract is known as anticipatory breach.

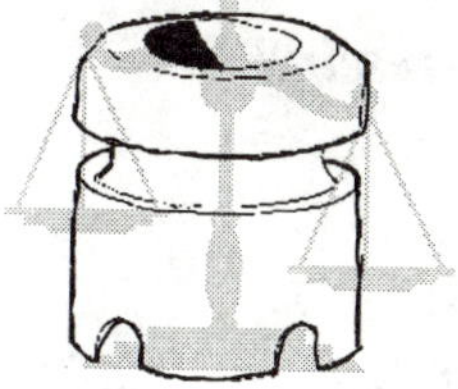

Same facts as above. On June 10, O refuses to make any payment (even the $65,000 that K has earned) and ejects K from the job.

O's action is legally justified. His obligation to make a payment on June 10 was excused by K's definite statement that he would stop work unless O paid K more than the amount he had earned.

14. Rescission

K is making normal progress constructing a hospital for O, when O misses a progress payment. After 20 days, K stops work.

K has the right to stop work because O has committed a material breach of contract. Now K has three options.

Option 1: K files suit for breach of contract.

K will recover the value of the work performed as measured by the contract price, plus the profit that K could have earned if permitted to finish.

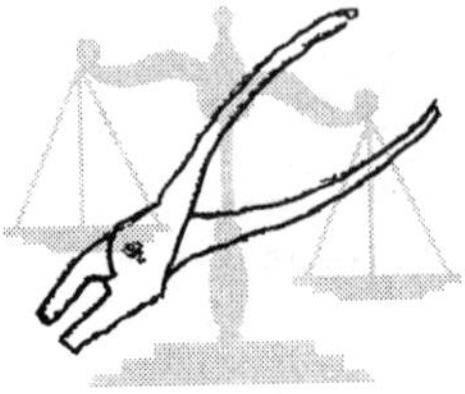

Option 2: K rescinds the contract.

Since O has committed a material breach, K may rescind (cancel) the contract.

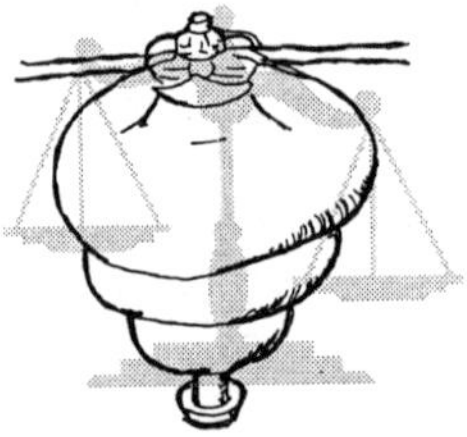

K sues O for restitution.

Now K can recover from O the reasonable value of the work performed even if it is more than the contract price.

Legalese. *The theory of the law is that when a contract has been rescinded, it is as if the contract had never existed. The aim of the law then is to restore the parties to the positions they occupied before the contract was signed. This process of restoration is called "restitution".*

In order to put K and O back where they were before the contract was signed, the law would like to return the construction work to K and take it away from O. This being impossible, the law does the next best thing which is to award to K the reasonable value of the construction work performed. Since K's award is not limited by the contract price, K, by canceling, can turn a losing contract into a profitable contract.

Option 3: K stops work, demobilizes, and remains ready, willing, and able to perform.

15. Owner's Damages for Delay

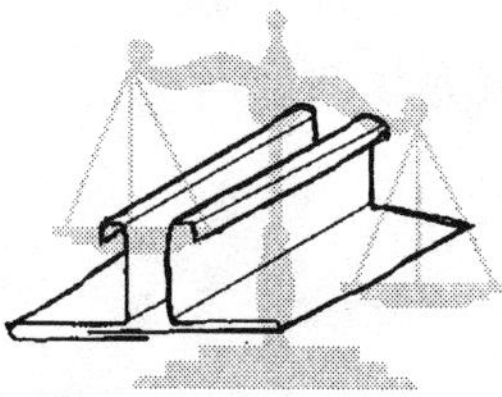

Contract requires K to complete construction of hospital in 20 months. Operating inefficiently, K finishes the job 100 days late. Interest on the hospital's construction loan is $7,300 per day. Hospital withholds $730,000 from K's final payment.

The daily interest on its construction loan is a valid measure of the hospital's damages for delay. This is because the hospital has paid the interest expense without the offsetting benefit of the use of the hospital.

16. Reasonable Rental Value

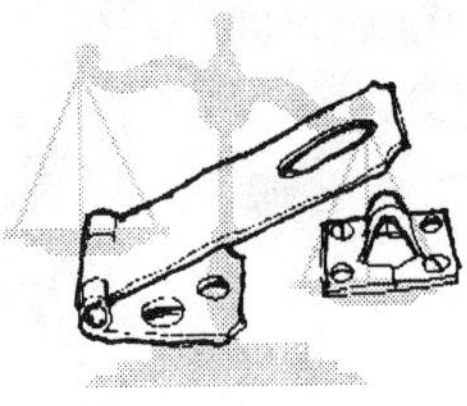

Same facts as above, except the project is an apartment building rather than a hospital. Rental value of the apartment complex is $10,000 per day. Owner withholds $1,000,000 from the final payment.

In the case of an apartment complex, the reasonable rental value of the complex (less operating expenses) would be a valid measure of the owner's damages for the delay in completion of the project.

17. Liquidated Damages Clauses

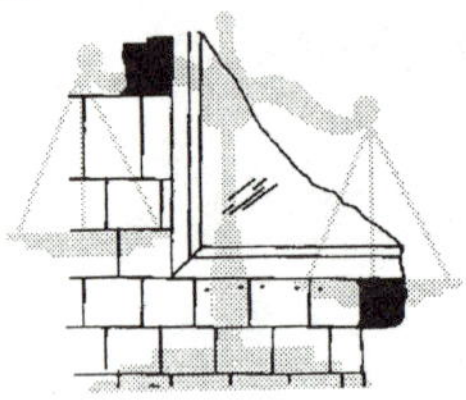

Same facts as above, except the contract provides that the contractor will pay the owner $1,000 per day as liquidated damages for delay in the completion of the project.

The owner is entitled to recover only $1,000 per day, even though its actual damages are greater.

18. Penalty Clauses

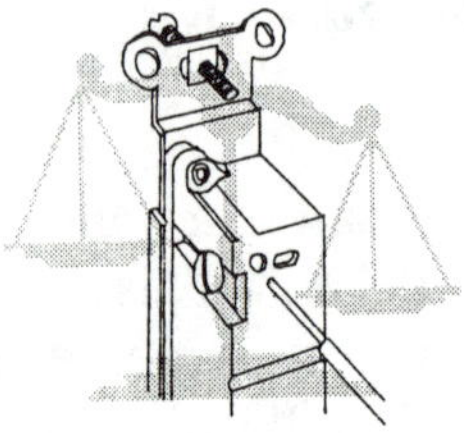

The contract provides that the contractor will pay a penalty of $20,000 for every day of delay.

Some states will not enforce "penalty" clauses. The rule in those states is that the owner may recover its actual damages, but not a "penalty".

19. Bonus Clauses

The contract provides for liquidated damages of $5,000 per day, but does not provide a bonus to the contractor for early completion.

A liquidated damages (predetermined damages) clause is enforceable even if there is no bonus clause in the contract.

20. Contractor's Damages for Delay

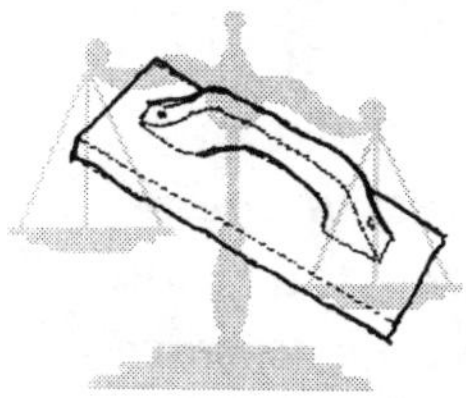

Hospital construction contract provides that owner will supply and install the medical gas system. Project is delayed for 100 days because owner fails to install the system on schedule.

Contractor may recover damages for delay. This includes field overhead (superintendent, general foreman, clerk of the works, field office expenses) and home office overhead (the percentage of home office overhead allocated to the job based on billings during the performance period).

Legalese. *The Eichleay formula divides the contractor's billings on a disputed contract by the total of all the contractor's billings during the* *performance period of the job, and applies the percentage thus obtained against the total home office overhead during the period of the project to compute the proportion of the total home office overhead that can be charged to the project. Total overhead is then divided by the number of days consumed in performance of the project to obtain the daily overhead, and the daily overhead is multiplied by the number of days of delay to produce the damages.*

---

21. Foreseeable Damages

O fails to make a progress payment to K and as a result K is unable to make a payment that is due to the IRS. The IRS levies on K's bank account, and K is forced to take bankruptcy. K sues O for the money it could have made over the next ten years if it had been able to stay in business.

Such damages are not recoverable because it was not foreseeable at the time when O and K signed the contract that failure to make a progress payment would cause K to become insolvent.

Legalese. *The rule that only foreseeable damages are recoverable in an action for breach of contract is known as the rule of Hadley v Baxendale, after an old English case in which the failure of a coach to arrive on schedule caused unanticipated damages. The rule of damages for tort causes of action is more generous to the* *plaintiff. In such cases, the plaintiff may recover full compensation for its injury even though the extent of damages might have been unforeseeable.*

Case in Point

A Kansas court has held that a contractor who agreed to build a bridge was required to finish the job at its own expense even though the bridge burned down when it was almost finished. The stipulated price contract made the contractor responsible for all foreseeable damage to the project, regardless of fault. The weather was dry. Flammable tarpaulins were used and dry creosote poles were on the jobsite. Despite foreseeable fire danger, the contractor permitted workers to smoke on the project. The bridge caught fire. The contractor did not have any firefighting equipment available. The bridge was destroyed. The court held that the contractor had the obligation to rebuild the bridge but no right to receive additional compensation from the owner. Reece Construction Co v State Highway Commission, 6 Kan App 2d 188 (1981).

CHAPTER 5

TORTS

18. Proximate Cause

19. Multiple Causes

20. Injury to Trespasser

21. Attractive Nuisance

22. Assumption of the Risk

23. Release

24. Release II

25. Workers Compensation Release

26. Independent Contractor

27. Ultra Hazardous Activity

28. Peculiar Risk Doctrine

29. Economic Loss

CHAPTER 5

TORTS

1. Negligence

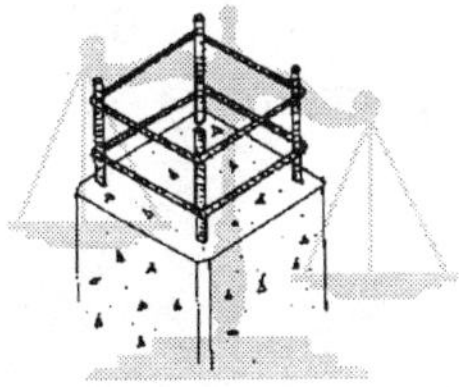

D (defendant), working on a crowded jobsite, carelessly backs up his pickup truck without looking, runs into P (plaintiff), and injures her.

D is liable to P for her damages including lost wages, medical expenses, disability, and pain and suffering. All persons must be careful (exercise due care) to avoid injury to others.

2. Vehicle Liability

The registered owner of the pickup is D-2 (defendant #2).

D-2 is also liable. The owner of a motor vehicle, even if not negligent, is liable for injuries it causes.

3. Indemnity, Vehicles

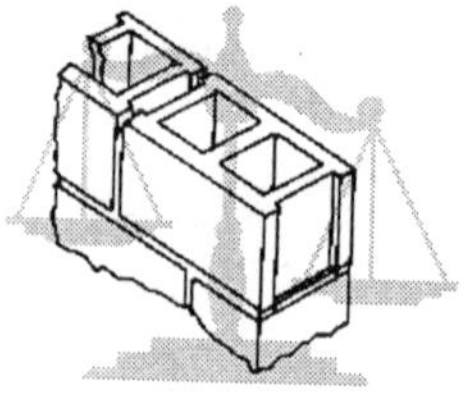

D-2 pays a judgment to P, and then seeks indemnity from D.

D-2 is entitled to indemnity (entitled to be held harmless). The accident was D's fault, and not D-2's fault.

4. Insurance

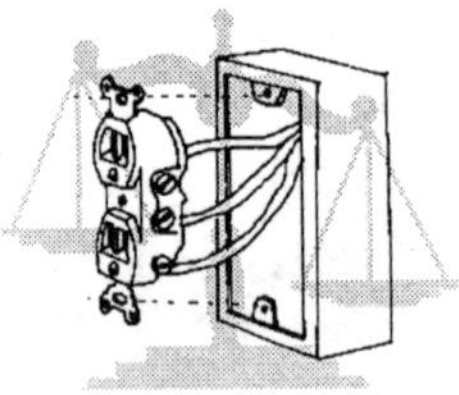

D-2's insurance company pays the judgment.

This is what usually happens because most vehicle owners carry liability insurance.

5. Subrogation

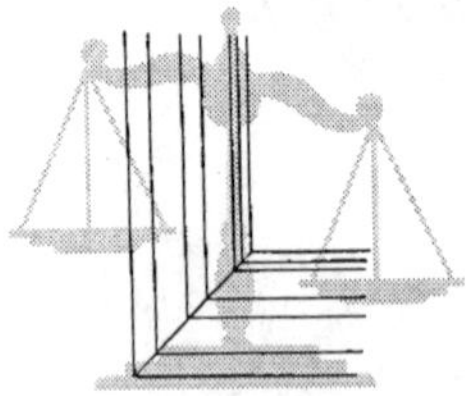

D-2's insurance company seeks indemnity from D.

Indemnity is allowed.

Legalese. Indemnity sought by a liability insurance company against a wrongdoer is known as "subrogation". A right to subrogation arises when an insurance company pays a judgment against its insured (or settles a claim against its insured), and thereby steps into the shoes of an insured who would have had a right to recover indemnity from a wrongdoer.

6. Subrogation Against Insured

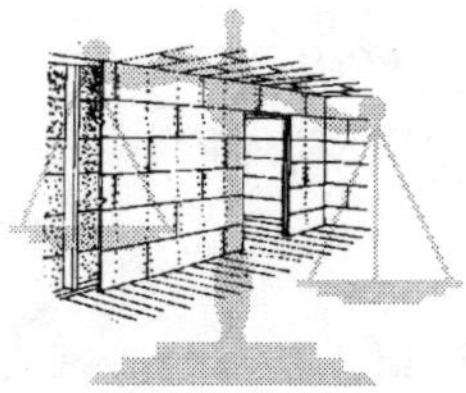

The insurance policy also provides insurance covering the potential liability of permissive users of the pickup.

In this case, the insurance company would not have indemnity rights against D because an insurance carrier cannot seek indemnity (subrogate) against its own insured.

7. Workers Compensation

P (plaintiff) was employed by K (prime contractor).

Under the workers compensation laws, K must pay P's medical expenses, lost earnings, and disability (but not for pain and suffering). Under workers compensation laws in effect in every state, an employer must compensate workers who are injured while on the job, even if he is not to blame for the injury.

8. The Exclusive Remedy Defense

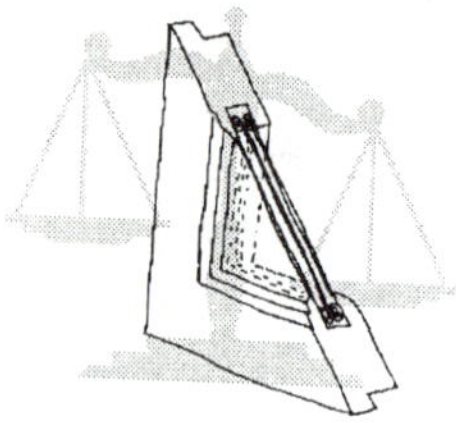

K's workers compensation carrier, WC, reimburses P for her medical expenses and lost wages and disability, but not for pain and suffering. P sues K, her employer, for pain and suffering, claiming K negligently supervised the project.

Since K is P's employer, and has paid her workers compensation, K is not liable for negligent supervision or for pain and suffering. Workers compensation is the employee's "exclusive remedy" against her employer.

Legalese. The workers compensation laws make an employer liable for workers compensation regardless of fault. In exchange for this, the workers compensation statutes exempt K from any claims by P except claims for workers compensation. P cannot sue K, her employer, for negligence.

---

9. Indemnity and the Exclusive Remedy Defense

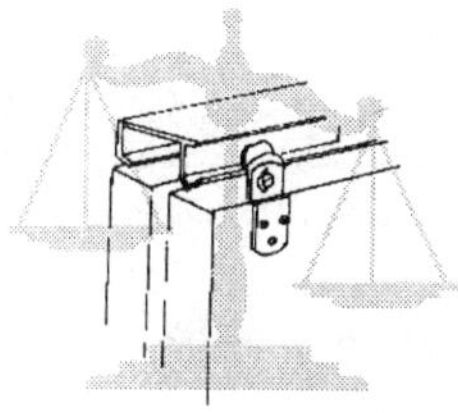

Same facts, with a subcontract provision requiring K (prime contractor) to indemnify S (subcontractor) against claims for bodily injury.

S may recover indemnity from K. The indemnity agreement prevails over the exclusive remedy defense.

10. Implied Indemnity and the Exclusive Remedy Defense

Same facts, but there is no indemnity agreement.

S, after paying P, may recover a share of the damages from K measured by the fault of K as compared to the fault of S in causing the injury to P. The exclusive remedy defense does not prevail over S's right to indemnity.

11. Acts of Employees

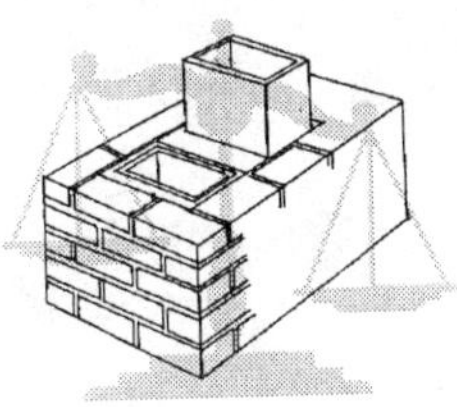

P (plaintiff) recovers judgment against S (subcontractor), the subcontractor that employed D, the driver of the pickup.

As D's employer, S is liable for damages caused by D in the course of employment.

Legalese. *Under a doctrine known as "respondeat superior", an employer is liable for the torts of its employee committed during the course of employment.*

---

12. Workers Compensation Lien

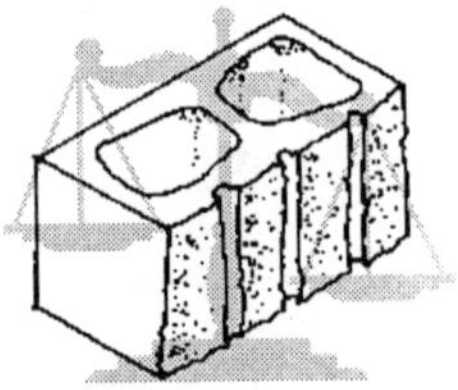

WC (workers compensation carrier) files a lien on P's judgment against S.

WC can enforce a workers compensation lien against any judgment recovered by P for damages caused by the injury for which the workers compensation was paid. This prevents P from obtaining a double recovery.

13. Recoupment by Employer

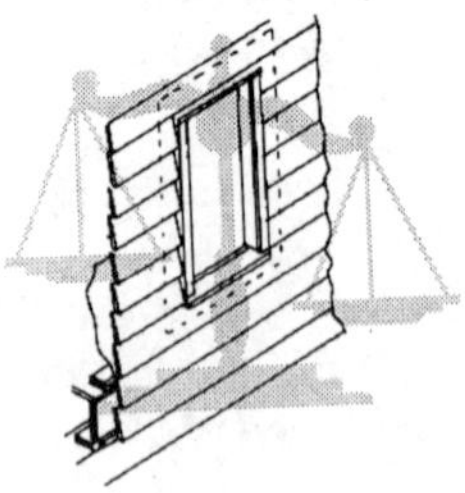

S (subcontractor) now sues D (driver) for indemnity.

An employer may recover indemnity from a negligent employee who causes an injury for which the employer is legally responsible.

14. Legal Duty

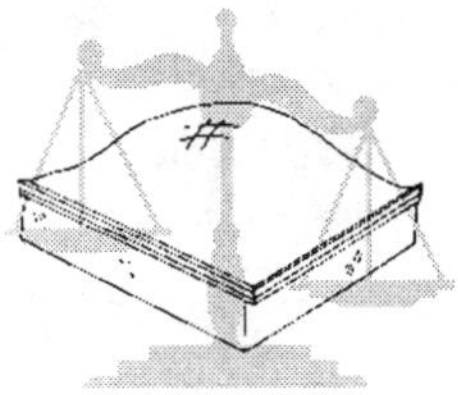

A (architect) inspects a jobsite to determine job progress under a written contract with O (owner). The contract provides that K (prime contractor) is responsible for jobsite safety and A has no such responsibility. A fails to notice that an employee of S (elevator subcontractor) has removed safety lines from a floor penetration. W (night watchman) falls into the penetration and is injured.

A is not legally responsible for W's damages because A was under no duty to inspect the jobsite for safety precautions. Both K and S are legally responsible: K because the contract made K responsible for jobsite safety, and S because its employee removed the safety line.

15. Jobsite Safety, Multiple Causes

Same facts as above, and W's injuries are aggravated because R (a rodbuster) left a piece of vertical rebar unprotected by a safety cap.

Here, R (and its employer) are also responsible for W's injuries.

16. Violation of Statute

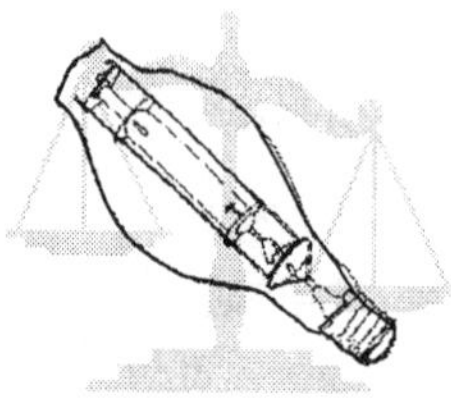

Building code requires wiring to be installed in rigid conduit. E (electrical contractor) installs Romex without rigid conduit. A short circuit in the Romex causes a fire.

E is legally responsible for any damage or injury caused by the fire. Violation of a statute is automatically deemed to be negligent conduct.

17. Purpose of Statute

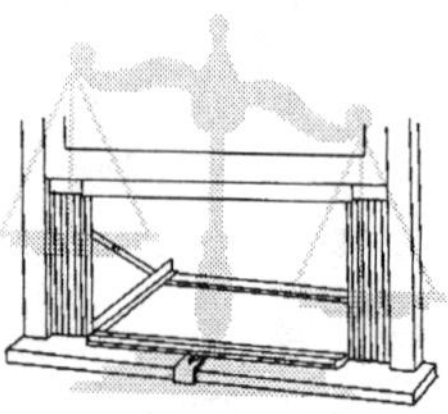

Same as above, but there is no fire. P (plaintiff) is injured when he trips over a roll of Romex stored at the jobsite.

Here, the violation of the statute would have no bearing on determining whether E was negligent or not. The purpose of the statute was not to prevent the type of injury sustained by P, but to suppress fire danger.

Legalese. *Violation of a statute enacted to protect against injury is "negligence per se". The negligence is only "actionable", however, if it is the legal ("proximate") cause of an injury to a person whom the statute was designed to protect against such injury.*

18. Proximate Cause

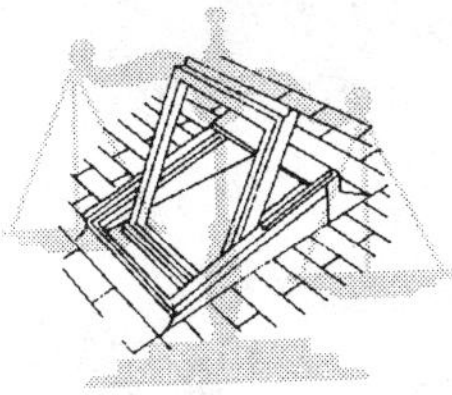

P (plaintiff) driving late at night, falls asleep, crashes through a barricade and into a trench that was dug by K (contractor). P sues K for damages.

P argues that the damages were caused by K since, if K had not dug the trench, P would not have been injured. Nevertheless, the digging of the trench was not the legal (proximate) cause because K's conduct was not negligent. The legal cause was P's own negligence in falling asleep at the wheel.

19. Multiple Causes

S (subcontractor) digs a trench across a sidewalk and leaves it properly barricaded. An employee of K (prime contractor), who has responsibility for barricading the entire jobsite, removes the barricade. P (pedestrian), walking at night, falls into the trench.

Although the accident would not have happened but if the trench, had not been dug by S, the legal cause is the negligence of K's employee, who removed the barricade.

20. Injury to Trespasser

P, while burglarizing a construction site at night, steps on a nail and injures his foot.

P cannot recover damages from the owner of the project because a property owner has no duty to protect trespassers from injury.

21. Attractive Nuisance

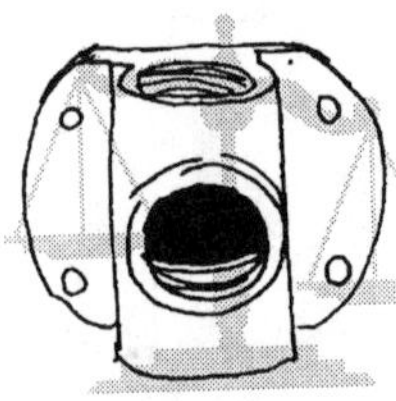

Children play hide and seek on an unfenced construction site on the way home from school. One is injured by stepping on a nail.

Here, the injured child may recover damages from the property owner. The owner should foresee that children may not be able to resist the temptation to use a construction site as a playground, and should take precautions to protect them from injury.

Legal Lore

Many states have passed laws to encourage the owners of property with recreational values to allow members of the public to use the property. Under such laws, owners who do not fence their recreational property are protected from injury claims.

22. Assumption of the Risk

A baseball spectator sitting near home plate is injured by a foul ball.

Such a spectator takes the risk of injury from known and obvious dangers associated with the sport, and therefore has no legal claim for damages.

23. Release

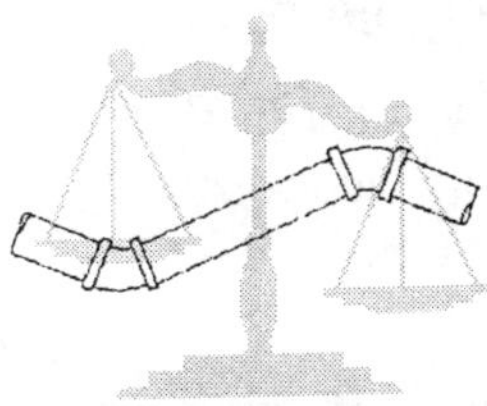

A novice skydiver is shown a video that emphasizes the dangers of the sport. The tape admonishes that there no such thing as a perfect pilot, a perfect airplane, a perfect parachute, or a perfect skydiving instructor. She signs a form releasing the skydiving school from liability, and initials a paragraph acknowledging that she knows she may die if she jumps out of an airplane at 13,000 feet.

Such releases, signed by an adult, are effective.

24. Release II

A ticket purchased by a rock concert patron provides that the patron releases the concert management from all claims for bodily injury. Because of inadequate security measures, the patron is injured in a riot.

Such a release will not stand up in court. Although the patron may have the release in her pocket, she has not agreed to its terms.

25. Workers Compensation Release

A carpenter who has been injured in a jobsite accident accepts a check for $1,000 from his employer in exchange for a written release of any workers compensation claims.

The release is ineffective. Release of workers compensation rights by a worker is invalid unless approved by court order.

26. Independent Contractor

As we have seen, under the doctrine of respondeat superior, an employer is responsible for damages wrongfully caused by its employee in the course of employment. Courts have found that this is a necessary social policy because it makes those who profit from the work of the employee responsible for insuring a measure of public safety. A business owner may be able to avoid liability, however, by having the work done by an independent contractor rather than by an employee.

S (shipper) ships a parcel by Fed Ex. The driver parks the delivery van and leaves it unattended while delivering the parcel. The van rolls downhill and crashes into another vehicle.

S is not liable since Fed. Ex. was an independent contractor and not the employee of S.

Legal Lore

Distinction between employee and independent contractor: An employee performs work as instructed by the employer. An independent contractor is responsible for achieving a finished result, but the manner of achieving that result is not controlled by the person for whom the services are performed.

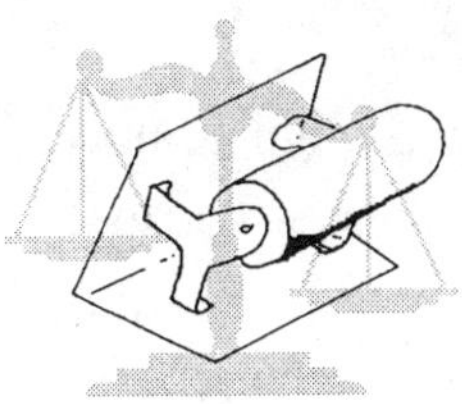

O (owner) signs a contract with K (contractor) under which K agrees to grade O's lot per plans and specifications.

K is an independent contractor because it has assumed responsibility to achieve a finished result, and the manner of performance is left up to K.

O (owner) rents a bulldozer from S (supplier) on an "operated and maintained" basis. The hourly rent paid by O includes the services of the bulldozer operator. The operator follows O's instructions as to where, when, and how to dig.

Here, the operator is legally classified as the "employee" of O because O retained control over the specific manner in which the work was performed. If the operator should negligently drive the bulldozer and injure a third party, O will be responsible for the injury.

27. Ultra Hazardous Activity

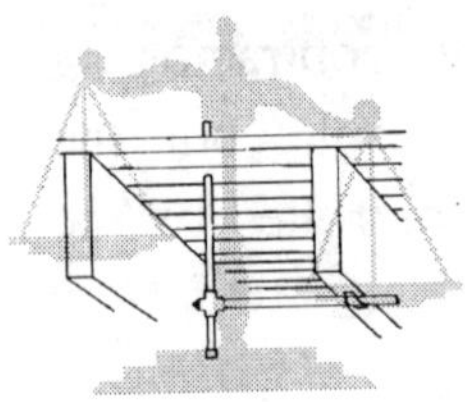

O (owner) employs K (blasting contractor) to perform road work. P (plaintiff) is injured in a blast set by K.

Here, O is liable for the injury even though K may have been an independent contractor. This is because blasting is recognized as an "ultra hazardous" activity. A property owner who utilizes blasting is engaging in such a dangerous activity that the law does not allow it to shield itself from liability by hiring an independent contractor.

28. Peculiar Risk Doctrine

In the last half century American courts have gradually, step-by-step, developed law to support a social policy that those profit from a business should bear the burden of injuries caused by that business. The doctrine that a person is not responsible for torts committed by an independent contractor exempted, in many cases, the beneficiaries of economic activity from the degree of responsibility felt by the courts to be appropriate.

Thus, for social policy reasons, the doctrine of ultra hazardous activity expanded so much that a new name had to be found. The new name is *peculiar risk.*

Consider the case of the owner of a factory with a leaky roof. To repair the leaks, someone will have to go up on the roof. It's always possible that a person working on a roof may fall from it. Fixing a roof isn't necessary as dangerous as setting off dynamite, but nevertheless there is a special risk associated with working on a roof, and it is the owner of the factory who benefits from the risk taken by the worker who climbs up.

To deal with situations of this type, courts gradually developed the peculiar risk doctrine.

The doctrine in some states has gone so far that it almost always applies to impose liability on a property owner for injuries to workers employed by independent contractors unless some special reason is found not to apply the doctrine.

The doctrine requires that a property owner who employs an independent contractor to perform operations that the property owner should recognize as involving a peculiar risk of harm to workers employed upon the project is legally responsible for a failure to prevent such harm from occurring. Such activities as roofing, painting, erection of scaffolding, raising walls, and trenching have been held to involve a peculiar risk. Courts reason that a property owner, exposed to such potential liability, will be unlikely to employ an underfinanced and uninsured independent contractor.

The development of the doctrine appears to have had its intended effect, since it is now customary for owners who employ construction contractors to insist that they carry adequate liability insurance, and name the owners as "additional insured". In addition, property owners are advised to carry adequate backup liability insurance on their own account to provide coverage for claims that may be made by persons injured on a construction project.

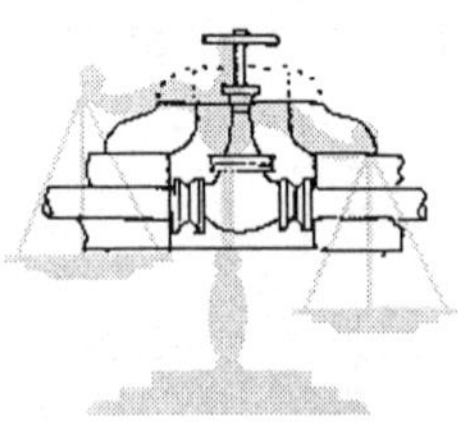

O (owner) employs K (contractor) to repair a factory roof. O requires K to purchase an endorsement under which O is named as an additional insured on K's commercial general liability insurance policy. W (worker) falls from the roof and is injured.

Here, W will collect workers compensation insurance for medical expenses, disability, and loss of earnings from K's workers compensation carrier. Since workers compensation is the exclusive remedy against K, W cannot sue K for damages, but sues O for damages under the peculiar risk doctrine. The workers compensation carrier is given a lien against any judgment W may recover from O, and the balance of the judgment will be paid to W. O, as an additional insured, will be defended against W's claim by K's liability insurance carrier.

Thus the social policy is served because the expense of compensating for W's injury is imposed on K and O, who realized economic benefit from W's work. The expense was imposed on K and O by means of insurance premiums paid by K and passed on to O as a part of the contract price. Since insurers adjust their premiums according to loss ratios, K is strongly motivated to run a safe jobsite in order to be able to buy insurance at competitive rates.

29. Economic Loss

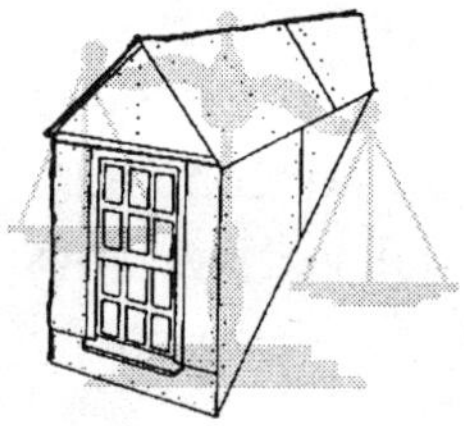

The roof of a warehouse leaks. Clothing stored in the warehouse is damaged. The owner of the warehouse incurs the expense of repairing the leaks.

The damage to the clothing is known as "property damage". The cost of repair is known as "economic loss".

"Economic loss" is expense incurred because of the failure of a product or structure to perform so as to give the owner the economic benefit that the owner expected to realize.

A controversial issue in the field of construction law is whether economic loss is a type of damage that can be recovered in an action for negligence or malpractice. In many states, the courts have held that economic loss cannot be recovered in the absence of a contractual relationship.

The exterior wood surfaces of a condominium become unsightly, warped, and cracked because of water intrusion. Condominium owners sue the project architect for malpractice, alleging failure to specify a proper vapor barrier.

In states that recognize the doctrine of economic loss, the architect will not be liable to the condominium owners because the type of damage alleged, dealing with the value and utility of the product purchased by the condominium owners, is economic loss.

Case in Point

An apartment dweller suffered second and third degree burns after he got into a bathtub without first testing the water temperature. A New York court held that the contractor who had installed the hot water system was liable to the tenant because he failed to provide proper controls to prevent hot water from reaching dangerous temperatures. Tirella v American Properties Team, Inc, 435 NYS2d 252 (1988).

CHAPTER 6

FRAUD AND MISREPRESENTATION

1. Opinion
2. Statement of Fact
3. Negligent Misrepresentation
4. Belief
5. Reliance
6. Promissory Fraud
7. Interference
8. Employer Liable
9. Own Contract
10. Interference with Prospective Economic Advantage
11. Competition Privilege
12. Diversion of Funds

CHAPTER 6

FRAUD AND MISREPRESENTATION

1. Opinion

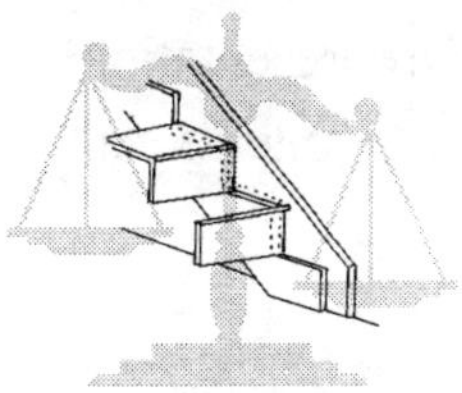

D (developer) tells H (homebuyer) "this house is worth $100,000." H, believing D's statement, purchases the house for $90,000. It is proved by an appraiser that the house is only worth $75,000. H sues D for $15,000.

Judgment for D. Statements of opinion are not fraudulent.

2. Statement of Fact

Same parties, but D tells H "this house is built on natural ground." H, believing D's statement, buys the house. Actually, as D knows, the house is built on fill, which settles.

Here we have a false statement of fact, relied upon by H, who, as a result of the reliance, suffered damage. D is legally responsible to pay H for the damages.

3. Negligent Misrepresentation

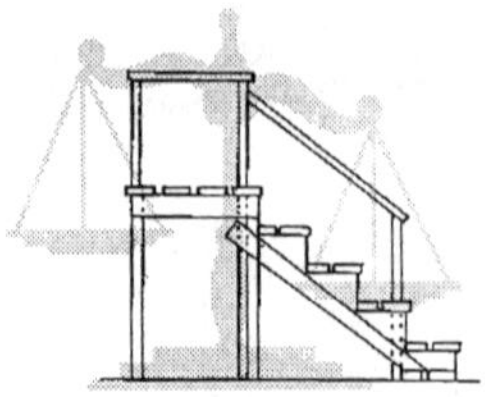

Same facts, but D did not actually know that the house was built on fill. The information, however, was readily available to a developer in D's position.

Judgment for H. A negligent misrepresentation (false statement) is illegal, as is an intentional misrepresentation.

Legal Lore

Intentional misrepresentation (fraud) will support an award of punitive damages, while negligent misrepresentation will not support such an award.

4. Belief

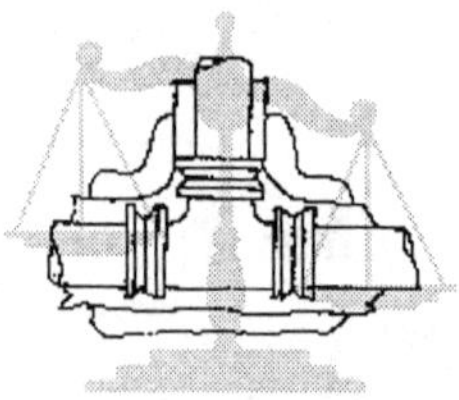

Same parties. D: "This is house is plumbed with copper pipe." H, examining the house, learns that it is plumbed with steel pipe, but buys the house anyway.

H has no cause of action for fraud, because H was not actually fooled.

5. Reliance

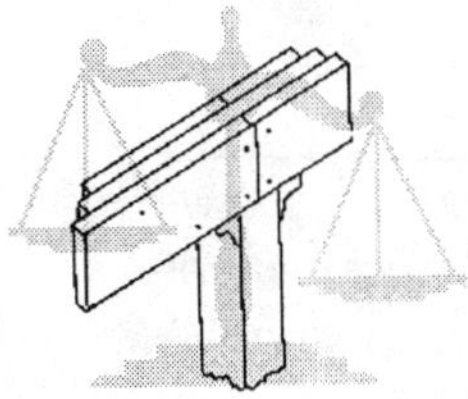

Same parties. D falsely represents that a house is plumbed with copper pipe. H does not buy the house.

H has no cause of action for fraud because H did not take any action in reliance upon the misrepresentation.

Legal Lore

The elements of a cause of action for fraud are 1) a false representation of fact, 2) known by the defendant to be false. 3) Plaintiff believes, 4) relies upon the false misrepresentation, 5) and suffers damages because of that reliance.

6. Promissory Fraud

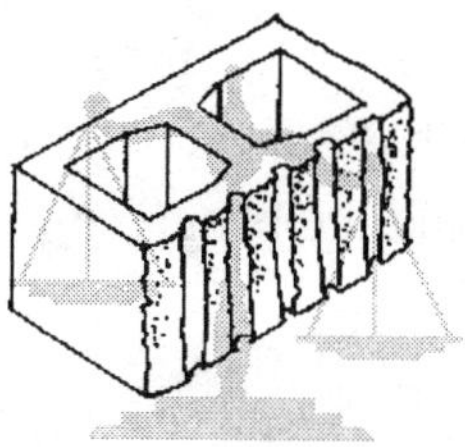

K (contractor) contracts to build a house for O for $150,000, and to finish the job by June 1. Actually, K knows that he cannot finish the job by June 1 and has no intention of completing the job for $150,000, but expects to make the job profitable by making unreasonable charges for extra work.

K has committed fraud by making a promise that he does not intend to keep.

Legalese. *This type of fraud is known "promissory fraud", or "fraud in the inducement of a contract". Promissory fraud carries punitive damages.*

---

7. Interference

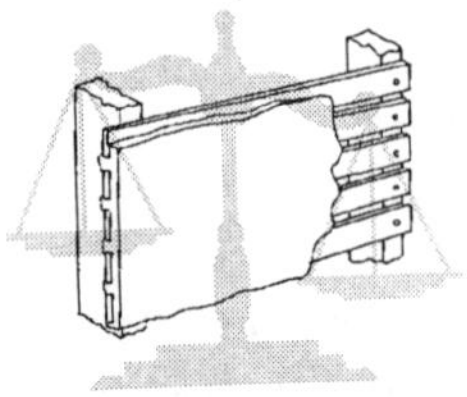

I (inspector), an employee of engineer, knows that the door hardware provided by K (contractor) for a school job complies with the requirements of the specifications, but nevertheless rejects it. O (owner) withholds progress payments until K upgrades the door hardware as demanded.

This is an example of a tort known as "intentional interference with contract". In effect, I has induced O to breach its contract with K by withholding progress payments even though K was entitled to be paid.

8. Employer Liable

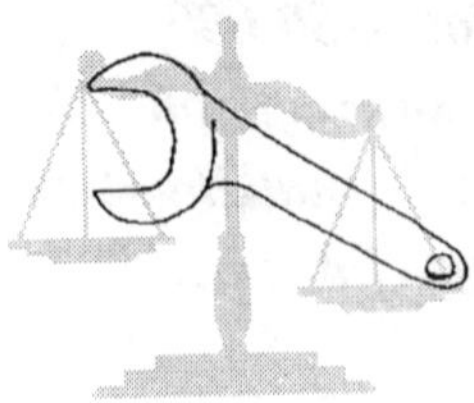

Same as above, K (contractor) files suit against E (engineer).

Judgment for K. In rejecting the hardware, the inspector was acting in the course and scope of her employment, as an employee of the engineer.

9. Own Contract

Same as above, but I is an employee of O (owner), rather than an employee of E (engineer).

Here, O has breached the contract but I has not committed the tort of intentional interference with contract. It is legally impossible for a party to interfere with its own contract.

10. Interference with Prospective Economic Advantage

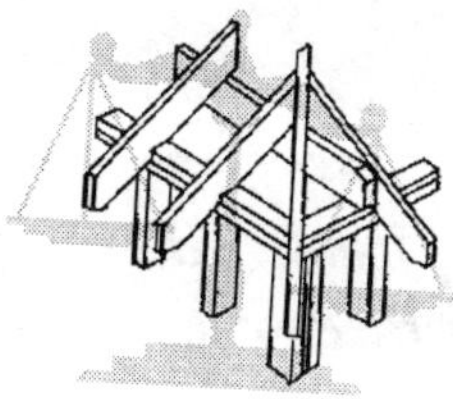

For ten years K (contractor) buys his construction bid bonds and performance bonds from A (bond agent). K and A fall into an argument about personal matters and K takes his business elsewhere. A, motivated by anger and hatred, and intending to damage K's bonding capacity, lets it be known around the surety industry that K is a bad risk. K sues A for the profits he could have realized if he could have made bond.

K has a good cause of action for "intentional interference with prospective economic advantage" (sabotaging a potential good deal).

11. Competition Privilege

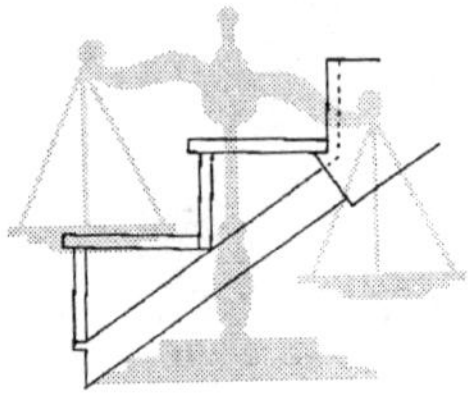

K-1 and K-2 (contractors) compete with each other for a warehouse job. K-2 informs O (owner) that K-2 is better qualified to perform the project than K-1. K-2 is motivated by hatred for K-1, who is a former employee of K-2.

No cause of action. Contractors are legally allowed to compete with each other for business and to express their opinions about the competition. No amount of evil intent will make such a statement unlawful.

12. Diversion of Funds

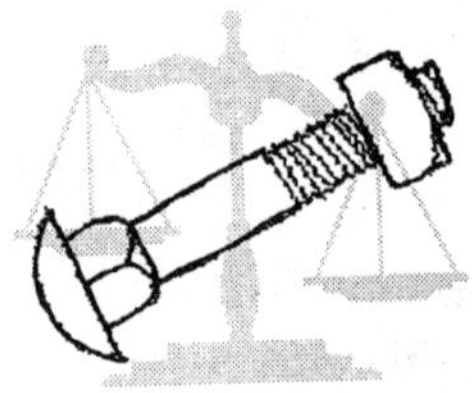

K (contractor) uses a progress payment from O (owner) to buy a new racehorse. The horse runs out of the money, K becomes insolvent and cannot pay for materials. M (material supplier), unpaid, records a mechanics lien on O's property.

K is guilty of an offense. In many states, such a diversion of funds constitutes the crime of theft, and is treated like larceny or embezzlement. In such a case, O could recover punitive damages from K. K could face imprisonment for theft.

Case in Point

A California builder contracted to design and build an outdoor patio and living area in an owner's rear yard for $5,671. When he submitted plans to the building department they were disapproved because of code violations. The builder submitted a new set of plans which were approved and a permit was issued. The builder then, without telling the owner, built to the original plans rather than to the corrected plans. The court held that the builder was liable for fraud and awarded punitive damages to the owner plus compensatory damages for the cost of restoring the property to the original condition after the building department red-tagged the job. Kuchta v Allied Builders Corp, 21 Cal App 3d 541 (1971).

CHAPTER 7

WARRANTY AND STRICT LIABILITY

CHAPTER 7

WARRANTY AND STRICT LIABILITY

1. Implied Warranty

O (owner) buys a house from a developer. Through no fault of the developer, the slab cracks.

Developer must pay O's damages under the doctrine of implied warranty.

Legalese. *A merchant builder who sells new houses is bound by the doctrine of implied warranty, under which the law implies a warranty that the structure is fit for its intended purpose. In the case of housing, this is known as "implied warranty of habitability". An implied warranty arises in the absence of any written warranty. If the builder also makes an express written warranty, the written warranty is controlling over any implied warranty.*

Under the Uniform Commercial Code (UCC), which governs the law of sales a sale of goods automatically carries an "implied warranty of merchantability" and an "implied warranty of fitness for a particular purpose."

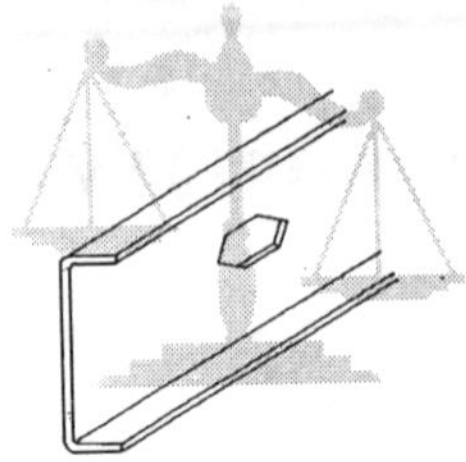

B (buyer) purchases a vacuum cleaner from S (seller). The motor burns out after a few hours of use.

Here, the vacuum cleaner was not of merchantable quality and it was not suitable for the purpose of housecleaning because the motor didn't work. Therefore B is entitled to compensation under the doctrine of implied warranty.

2. Strict Liability

The plaintiff, O-2 (second owner) who purchased a home from the original owner, makes a claim against developer for a cracked slab.

The doctrine of "strict liability" protects used homebuyers owners as well as the original homebuyer.

Legalese. *The doctrine of strict liability (sometimes known as "products liability") applies to housing manufacturers just as it does to the manufacturers of other products. The doctrine applies in favor of consumers to protect them against damages from defective products even if there was no negligence or other wrongful conduct in the manufacture or construction of the product.*

---

3. Non Consumer

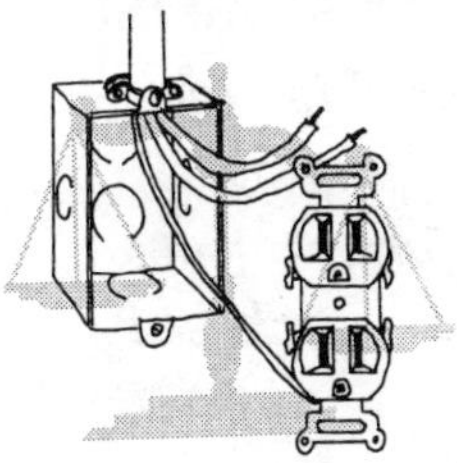

After the slab cracks, the discouraged homebuyer moves out and stops making payments on the mortgage. The bank forecloses, repairs the slab, and claims damages from the developer.

The doctrine of implied warranty only protects buyers. D is not liable to the bank because it was not negligent and because the doctrine of strict liability applies only to protect consumers, and not financial institutions.

4. Foreseeability

Developer improperly compacts fill, sells house to owner, slab cracks, owner abandons the house and stops making payments on the mortgage, bank forecloses and sues developer for damages.

Here, the developer could have foreseen that improper compaction would cause the slab to crack which would cause a homebuyer to abandon the house which would cause the bank to foreclose and suffer damages. Judgment for the bank.

5. Negligence and Strict Liability

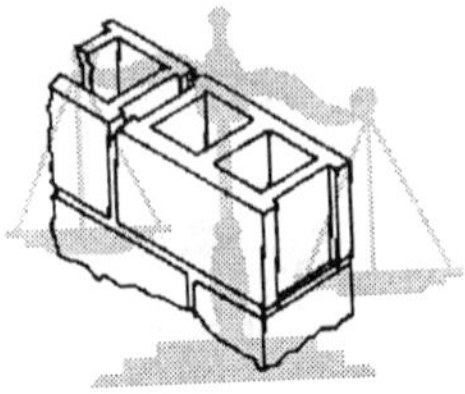

The slab was caused to crack by fill that was improperly compacted by the farmer from whom the developer purchased the property.

Here, the farmer is not legally responsible to pay damages if it was not foreseeable by the farmer that the fill, if improperly compacted, would cause future damage to some homebuyer.

Legalese. *The farmer is not liable under the doctrine of implied warranty because he did not sell the house to plaintiff, and is not liable under the doctrine of strict liability because he is not a merchant builder. He also is not liable under the doctrine of negligence because his careless actions did not cause foreseeable damages.*

---

6. Express Warranty

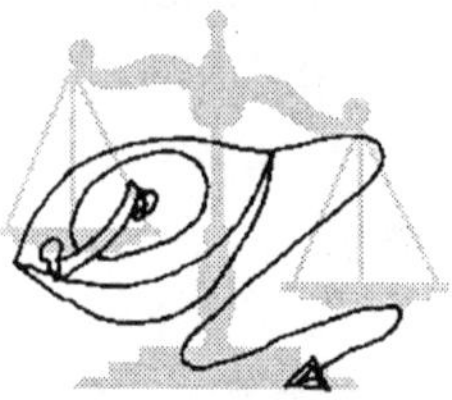

B buys a vacuum cleaner from S, who gives to B a written warranty against defects. After three hours of use, the motor burns out.

Here, B may receive compensation under the doctrine of express warranty as well as under the doctrine of implied warranty. A written warranty given by a seller to a buyer is called an express warranty while an implied warranty arises automatically from the very occurrence of the sales transaction.

O (owner) employs R (roofer) to install a roof with a ten-year warranty issued by M (manufacturer of roofing materials). R installs the roof and delivers to O a written warranty issued by M. Three years after installation, the roof begins to leak because the roofing material disintegrates in the sun. The leaks cause $100,000 in damages to television sets stored in the building.

O may recover compensation from M under the express warranty including the cost of repairing the roof and the damage to the television sets.

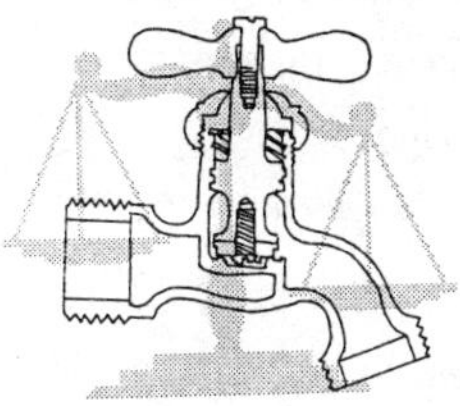

Same as above, but the warranty issued by M expressly excluded liability for consequential damages.

Here, O could recover from M the cost of roof repairs but not for the damages to the television sets or other such damages.

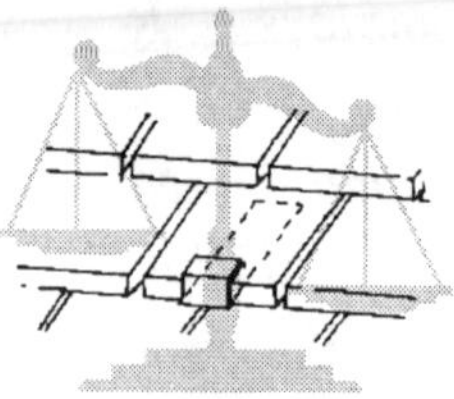

Same as above, but M had distributed advertising materials to O's architect (A) who specified M's material based on representations in the advertising material that M's product was impervious to sun damage.

Here, O may recover all damages from M because the express warranty made by M to A is enforceable by O, since O, the buyer, was the final target of the warranty, and the express warranty contained in the advertising material did not limit liability for such damages.

7. Warranty and Indemnity

Same as above, but the selection of roofing material was made by R (roofer) rather than A (architect). The contract between O and R provides that all materials used by R will be new, first class, and the best of their respective kinds.

Here, O may recover all damages from S because S breached the contract by supplying inferior roofing materials. S, in turn, may recover indemnity from M under the legal doctrine of "implied indemnity." This doctrine divides liability among defendants according to their share of fault. Since the loss was caused by defective materials rather than by defective contract performance by S, M must pay S for its liability to O.

8. Warranty and the Statute of Limitations

"Warranty" and the "statute of limitations" are both legal concepts that deal with time, and for that reason they are often confused. An written warranty extends legal rights for a specified time, while a statute of limitations cuts off legal rights after a specified time has gone by.

B (builder) builds a house for O (owner) under a contract that includes a one-year warranty against defective work and materials. Two years after the completion of construction, the roof begins to leak because of failure to properly caulk sheet metal flashing. B refuses to repair the roof, asserting that the one-year warranty has expired.

O is entitled to have the roof repaired. The improper caulking was a breach of contract. O has the right to file an action against B until expiration of the statute of limitations. (Limitations periods vary from state to state.)

The fact that the contract provided a one-year warranty neither shortens the statute of limitations nor nullifies a breach of contract.

Same as above, but construction is completed in 1997. The roof begins to leak in 2001. O files suit against B in 2003.

O has a good cause of action. The statutory period does not begin to run until O discovers (or should discover) breach.

Exactly what, one may ask, (if anything), does the one-year warranty add to the owner's rights?

Is the one-year warranty just a device used by contractors to hoodwink owners? There's more to it than that. The purpose of a one-year warranty is to require the contractor to fix anything that goes wrong regardless of fault. Thus, if doors and windows should stick even though constructed per plans and specs, in a diligent and workmanlike manner, and in compliance with trade practice, the contractor would still have fix them.

9. Products Liability

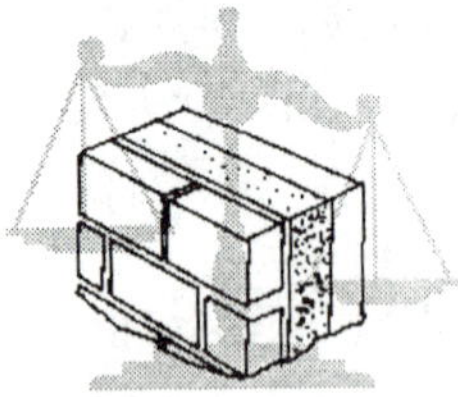

M (manufacturer) markets aluminum pipe as a product suitable for domestic plumbing. Beginning five years after installation, the pipe deteriorates and O-2 (owner), the second owner of a home in which the pipe was installed, must replace the plumbing system.

Does O have a claim against M? Let us assume that M was not negligent in the design or manufacture of the pipe but employed qualified metallurgists who complied with the standards of their profession in designing the piping materials. Therefore O has no tort claim against M.

O has no contractual rights against M since there is no contract between them.

O has no warranty rights against M since M made no express warranty.

As we have seen, the doctrine of implied warranty applies in the case of a sales transaction. But there was no sale between M and O. The house was sold to O by the original homeowner. So we have eliminated tort, contract, express warranty, and implied warranty as grounds of liability.

There remains, however, the concept of product liability (legalese: strict liability).

Under this doctrine, a manufacturer is liable to a consumer who suffers injury because of a defective product even if the product was manufactured with due care.

10. The Doctrine of Economic Loss

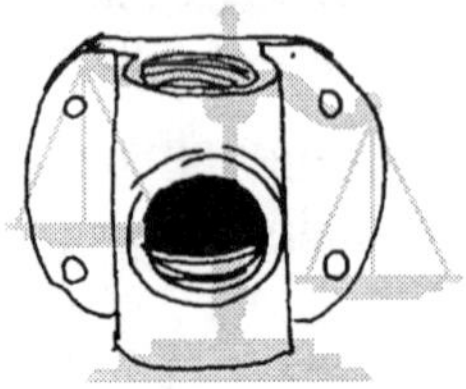

Same as above, but the leaks washed away the foundation and therefore O had to not only replace the plumbing system but repair damages sustained by the house when the foundation washed away.

Here, we encounter the doctrine of economic loss, which is in effect in about half of the states that have considered the question. "Economic loss" means loss sustained because of a failure of a product to meet the expectations of a consumer of that product as to efficiency, performance, and durability.

Here, O has sustained economic loss, because the market value of the house was reduced by the presence in it of defective piping. In states where the economic loss doctrine is applied, O would not recover from M this economic loss.

O, however, also suffered property damage when the foundation gave way and portions of the house collapsed. Since "property damages" is not "economic loss", O can recover those damages from M under the theory of products liability.

11. Implied Warranty of Plans

Contract specifies HVAC system in detail, including chillers, air handling units, motor sizes, dampers, and duct work. Contract provides that the system will reduce the ambient temperature by 30 degrees. Contractor installs the system as specified, but it only achieves cooling of 20 degrees.

No breach of contract. The owner gave the contractor an implied warranty that if the specifications were followed the desired cooling would be obtained.

Contract provides that contractor will obtain fill from borrow pit A. Borrow pit A is exhausted for the before required amount of fill is obtained. Contractor is required to import fill from borrow pit B, which is twice the distance.

Owner must reimburse contractor for the additional expense, since there was an implied warranty that borrow pit A contained sufficient material to perform the work.

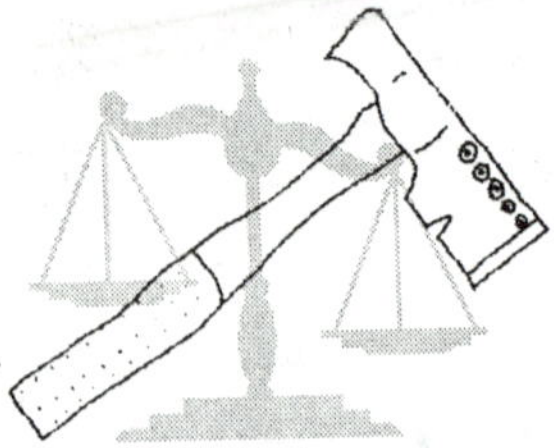

Hospital plans are full of conflicts between structural and mechanical elements so that duct work and piping are called out to occupy the same location as columns and girders. Mechanical subcontractors perform extensive extra work to make the systems fit. Prime contractor claims extra compensation from the owner to compensate the mechanical subcontractors for the extra work.

Owner must compensate the contractor breach of implied warranty that plans are properly prepared and buildable.

The prime contractor may "pass through" the claims of the mechanical subcontractors to the owner. The owner, in turn, may seek confirmation from the project architect who had responsibility for coordination of drawings.

Case in Point

A contractor learned the hard way that a one-year warranty does not protect a builder against claims for construction defects that occur more than one year after the completion of the project. A design-build contractor constructed a commercial building under a contract that provided he would remedy any defects due to faulty materials or workmanship which might appear within a period of one year from the date of final payment. The roof began to leak shortly after the one-year warranty expired and the contractor denied responsibility. The court entered judgment on a jury verdict of $13,687.92 against the contractor. A one-year warranty provision extends, rather than limits, a contractor's liability for faulty construction and in no way does it impair the contractor's general obligation to perform its work in a proper, workmanlike manner. The one-year warranty does not excuse a breach of contract just because the breach is not discovered until more than one year after the completion of the project. Burton-Dixie Corp v Timothy McCarthy Construction Co, 436 Fed 2d 405 (5th Cir 1971).

CHAPTER 8

CONSTRUCTION DEFECTS

CHAPTER 8

CONSTRUCTION DEFECTS

1. Breach of Contract

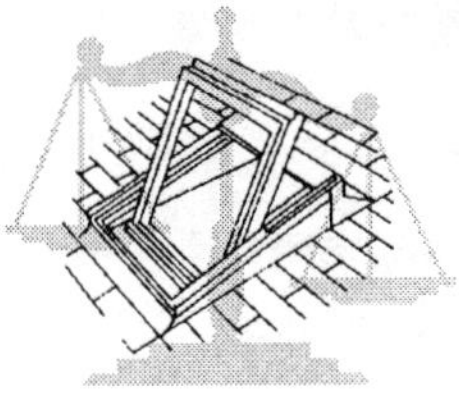

K (contractor) builds a warehouse for O (owner). The slab cracks. Investigation shows that S (grading subcontractor) did not properly compact the fill.

K is liable to O for damages for breach of contract. K is responsible for breaches by subcontractors.

2. Negligence

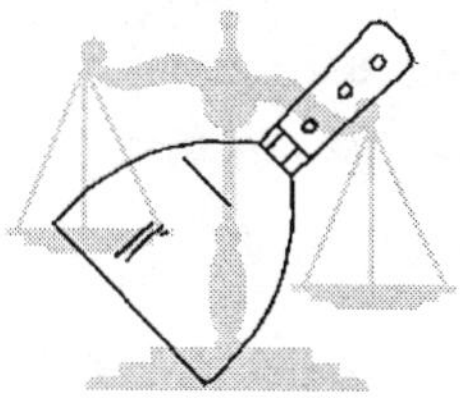

O (owner) claims damages both from S (grading subcontractor) and from K (prime contractor).

S is liable to O for the tort of negligence while K is liable to O for breach of contract.

3. Comparative Fault

It is determined that the cracking in the slab was caused partly by improper placement of reinforcing steel, which was installed at the bottom, rather than in the middle of the slab by S-2, concrete subcontractor.

Here, the jury will be asked to apportion fault between K, S, and S-2. Fault is apportioned according to percentages.

4. Contribution

Jury allocates fault to K (prime contractor)-- 10%; S (grading subcontractor)-- 40%; S-2 (concrete subcontractor)-- 50%. O collects the entire judgment from K.

K is entitled to recover contribution from S and S-2 according to their percentage of fault (40% of the amount of the judgment from S and 50% of the amount of the judgement from S-2, so that K ends up paying just 10% of the judgment).

5. Indemnity

Same facts, but S-2 (concrete subcontractor) has agreed to indemnify K against losses arising out of its performance of subcontract work even if the loss is partly K's fault.

The indemnity agreement controls, and K is entitled to recover 100% of the loss from S-2 rather than just a proportionate contribution.

Case in Point

The manufacturer of a roof membrane had to pay $1,000,000 in punitive damages because it continued to distribute specifications that were known to be defective. The manufacturer marketed its roofing materials by distributing product descriptions and model specifications to architects. The model specifications recommended the use of the roofing membrane over Zonolite (a lightweight insulating concrete) even though the manufacturer had experienced problems with that application and even though the employees of the manufacturer had recommended that the material should no longer be specified for use over Zonolite. Architects, relying on such publications, issued specifications calling for installation of the roofing membrane over Zonolite. The manufacturer inspected and approved the roof and issued a ten-year warranty. Almost immediately after the building was completed, the roof began to leak. The manufacturer disclaimed responsibility, claiming cracks in the roof membrane were caused by excessive moisture in the Zonolite. The court awarded $100,000 in compensatory damages and $1,000,000 in punitive damages to the building owner and against the manufacturer. The manufacturer learned of the recurring problems, and had a duty to change the specifications. The manufacturer willfully led architects to design expensive roofs which were neither durable, watertight, nor satisfactory. Stephen v Gaf Corp, 232 Kan 152 (1987).CHAPTER 9

INDEMNITY

CHAPTER 9

INDEMNITY

1. Indemnity Clause

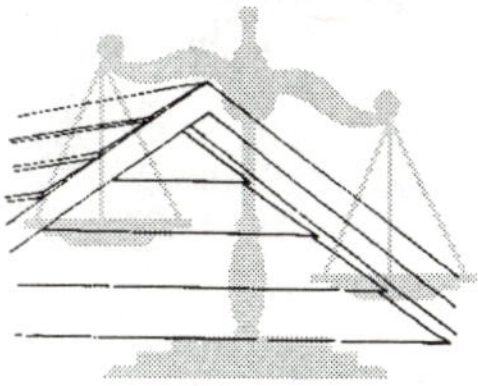

S (subcontractor) agrees to indemnify K (prime contractor) against claims arising out of S's performance of a plumbing subcontract. A plumber employed by S is injured when a scaffold erected by S collapses. The plumber sues K, claiming that K did not provide a safe work place.

K should call upon S to defend the lawsuit under the indemnity clause in the contract.

Legalese. *K would "tender the defense" to S.*

---

2. Duty to Defend

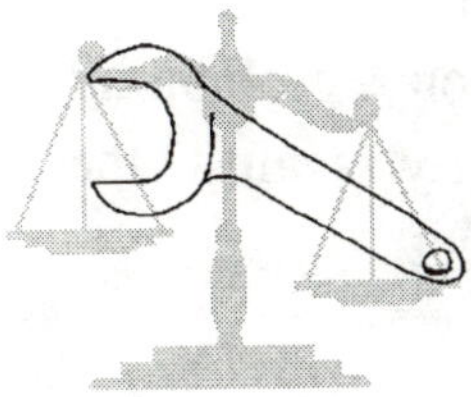

S refuses to pick up the defense.

K can recover judgment against S for the attorneys fees and expenses of defending the case, plus the amount of any judgment that the plaintiff might recover against K.

3. Misconduct of Person Indemnified

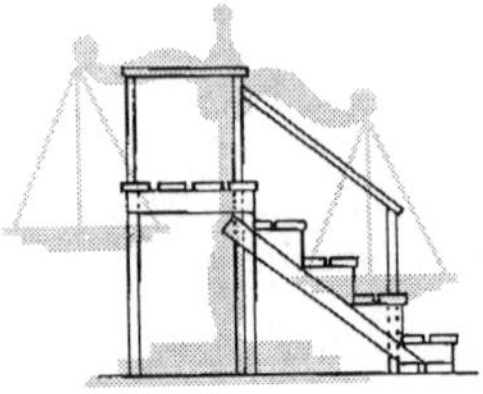

Same facts, except that collapsing scaffold was supplied by K, rather than S.

Here, the indemnity clause would not be enforceable because the accident was 100% K's fault.

4. Indemnity Against Sole Misconduct

Same facts, but the indemnity clause explicitly provides that S will indemnify K even against claims that are 100% K's fault.

In most states, such an indemnity clause is unenforceable because of legislation prohibiting indemnity clauses that protect a party against the consequences of its own, sole, misconduct.

5. Special Indemnity Clause

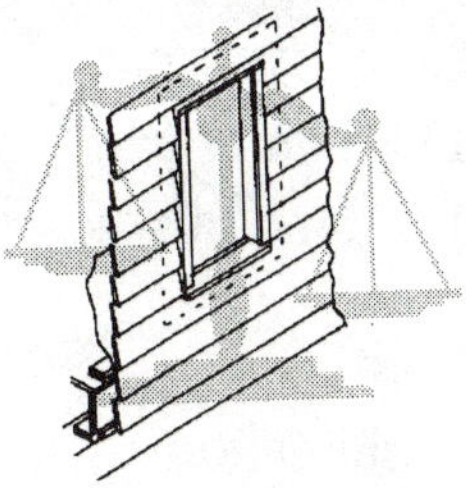

Inferior pipe installed by S fails after being stomped by an employee of K. O sues K and S for water damage and K calls upon S to defend the claim. The indemnity clause provides that S will indemnify K against claims caused in part by the misconduct of K.

The indemnity clause is enforceable, since K was not 100% at fault.

6. Indemnity Against Loss

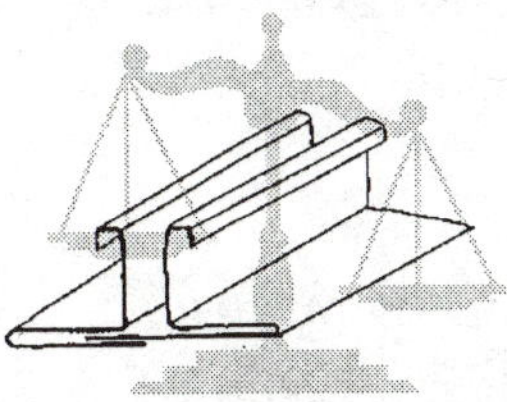

The indemnity clause does not mention claims. S agrees to indemnify K against losses.

Here, the indemnity clause gives K no rights against S until K has actually suffered a loss either by settling the claim or by paying a judgment obtained by the injured worker. K is not liable for the costs of defense.

Business Pointer

It is a good idea to submit indemnity clauses to your insurance carrier before signing the contract to determine whether a claim under the indemnity clause will be covered by your liability policies.

7. Indemnity Language

The language of an indemnity clause warrants careful attention because seemingly trivial variations can make a big difference in determining the amount of liability assumed by the indemnitor.

If an indemnity is against "loss" the obligation of the indemnitor arises only when the indemnitee has actually suffered a loss. To understand how restrictive this language is, consider that a defendant in a lawsuit may suffer much trouble and expense defending the suit, but it does not suffer an actual loss until it has paid the judgment. Once the judgment has been paid the duty to reimburse the loss arises.

On the other hand a defendant becomes liable, and the duty to hold harmless against "liability" arises, when judgment is entered.

If an indemnity is against "claims" or "demands," then the duty to hold harmless arises when a claim or demand is made. In such cases, the indemnitor has a duty, if called upon to do so, to provide a defense against the claims or demands.

A liability insurance policy is an example of an indemnity agreement. Most insurance policies give the insurance carrier not only the duty, but also the right, to defend the indemnitee (the insured) against claims and demands. The insured must take care to notify the carrier promptly when a claim or a demand is made so that the carrier may effectively exercise its right to provide a defense.

8. Statute of Limitations on Indemnity Agreements

Since the purpose of a statute of limitations is to prevent stale claims, the statutory time period for filing suit begins to run when a claimant has the right to sue.

***Legalese**. The legal expression for having a right to sue is to have a cause of action. A cause of action is said to arise when the claimant first has the right to sue. Therefore the statutory period begins to run when the plaintiff's cause of action arises.*

As a matter of simple logic, then, a cause of action arises for indemnity when the duty to hold harmless arises. The timing of that duty depends on the language of the indemnity agreement. If an indemnity is against "claims" or "demands," the duty arises when a claim or demand is made. If an indemnity is against "liability" the duty arises when the indemnitee becomes liable (when judgment is entered against the indemnitee). If an indemnity is against "loss," then the duty arises when the indemnitee has suffered a loss (paid off the judgment or claim).

S (subcontractor) has agreed to indemnify K (contractor) against any loss arising out of subcontractor's performance of work. S damages a car owned by C (claimant). C files suit against K in 1997 and recovers judgment in 2001. K pays the judgment in 2002.

The statute of limitations for filing an action to enforce a written contract is four years. K's right to sue S to enforce the indemnity agreement will not be barred by the statute of limitations until 2006.

This analysis can be important in practice. A person interested in purchasing S's business in 2004 should be aware of the possibility that a claim might still be asserted for an accident that occurred back in 1997.

9. Indemnity Clauses

Contractors should have their insurance agents review the language of indemnity clauses in contract documents under consideration. Indemnity clauses should be written with insurance coverage in mind, and a subcontractor's insurance policy should be designed to cover the subcontractor's obligation to indemnify a prime contractor. For this reason indemnity clauses recommended by insurance carriers usually concentrate on claims for bodily injury and property damage as defined in liability insurance policies. Other types of claims may, however, arise.

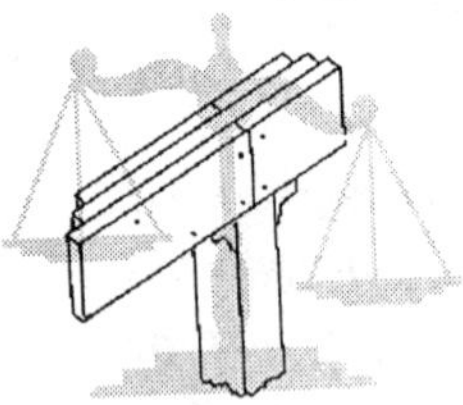

O (owner) makes a claim against K (prime contractor) for roof repairs under a ten year warranty of a roof installed by S (subcontractor).

This claim is not be for "property damage" as defined by a liability insurance policy, but an indemnity clause can be written so as to cover such claims, as well as claims for property damage.

10. The Duty to Defend and Conflict of Interest

O makes a claim against K for roof repairs under a ten year warranty. The roof was installed by S. K "tenders" the defense to S (calls upon S to defend K against the claim). S assigns L (lawyer), its regular lawyer, to defend the lawsuit filed by O against K and S. Upon investigation, S finds that the roof problems were caused by faulty framing, rather than by faulty roofing. S instructs L to file a cross-complaint against K.

The position of L here is untenable. A lawyer may not file a lawsuit against her own client. L must withdraw from the case and advise that K and S each to employ independent counsel. In order to fulfill the requirements of the indemnity agreement, S must pay the fees of both counsel.

Case in Point

An indemnity clause in a subcontract provided that the subcontractor would hold the owner harmless from any loss, expense, damage, demand, or claim arising out of bodily injury or property damage sustained by the owner in connection with performance of the work by the subcontractor. After the project was damaged by fire, the prime contractor on the project attempted to hold the subcontractor responsible under the indemnity agreement. The court held that the indemnity clause did not apply to the situation presented. The indemnity clause applies only to damages and losses arising out of claims made against the owner by third persons. For example, if a worker had been injured on the job and made a claim against the owner for bodily injury, the subcontractor may have been responsible to indemnify the owner against that claim. However, since the only damage suffered by the owner in this case was fire damage, and since no claim was being made against the owner, the indemnity clause did not apply. Varco-Pruden, Inc v Hampshire Construction Co, 50 Cal App 3d 654 (1975).

CHAPTER 10

INSURANCE

1. Types of Insurance
2. Builders Risk Insurance
3. All Risk Insurance
4. Liability Insurance
5. Broad Form
6. Subcontractor's Insurance
7. The Duty to Defend
8. Reservation of Rights
9. Progressive Loss
10. Efficient Cause

CHAPTER 10

INSURANCE

1. Types of Insurance

The construction industry is mainly interested in two types of insurance: property insurance and liability insurance.

Property insurance is to reimburses a property owner for damage caused by a casualty. This type of insurance pays a homeowner whose residence is damaged or destroyed by fire, flood, or earthquake.

Liability insurance, on the other hand, protects against *liability* for property damage or bodily injury done to some other person. A familiar example is insurance that protects the driver of an automobile against claims for damages arising out of a collision.

2. Builders Risk Insurance

Builders risk insurance is *property* insurance that is designed to insure the owner, the prime contractor, and subcontractors against damage to or destruction of a project by fire, flood, earthquake, or other peril, while the project is under construction.

Every well written construction contract should deal with damage to or destruction of the project and builders risk insurance. Several alternative schemes may be employed.

Under one scheme, damage to or destruction of the project relieves the contractor of the obligation of further performance, and the owner purchases whatever insurance the owner may think proper to protect himself against loss.

Under another scheme, the contractor must repair work that is damaged or destroyed during construction, and the contractor is required to purchase builders risk insurance to pay the cost of rebuilding.

Another scheme (this is the one adopted by the AIA contract documents) requires the owner to purchase builders risk insurance naming the owner as insured and contractor and subcontractors as "additional insureds." In the event of destruction of the project during construction the owner is required to collect the proceeds of insurance as trustee for the prime contractor and subcontractors, and use the proceeds of the insurance to pay for rebuilding.

The law excuses performance of a contract when performance becomes *impossible*. Contractors should be aware that performance of a construction contract is not excused by destruction of the project. Destruction of the project does not make performance impossible: it merely increases the expense of performance. A contractor should make sure that the contract either contains a clause that excuses performance if the project is destroyed, or requires one of the parties to purchase insurance against such a loss.

The position of a subcontractor is different. Destruction of a project usually does literally make the subcontractor's performance impossible. (It is impossible, for example, to hang drywall on a nonexistent frame.)

3. All Risk Insurance

Builders risk insurance is a form of "all risk" insurance, which means that the policy insures against all risks that are not specifically excluded from coverage. For example, many builders risk policies exclude loss caused by “earth movement” and by "faulty workmanship".

4. Liability Insurance

Most contractors carry a form of liability insurance known as *commercial general liability insurance*. The policy insures the contractor against liability for bodily injury and property damage. Many such policies also extend coverage for personal injury which, in insurance lingo, covers liability for such wrongs as false advertising, unfair competition, and unlawful eviction.

The typical commercial general liability (CGL) policy insures against physical injury to tangible property caused by accident. The most important exclusion from the standpoint of a contractor is the *work exclusion* which withholds coverage for damage to work performed by or on behalf of the insured contractor.

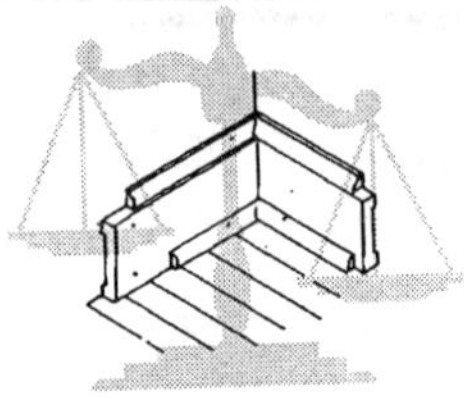

Five years after the completion of a warehouse project, the roof begins to leak. The leak causes damage to drywall, floor covering, and merchandise that is stored in the warehouse. O (owner) makes a claim against K (contractor) for the damage to the merchandise and the cost of repairing the roof, ceiling, drywall, and floor covering.

Since the work exclusion removes coverage for damage to work performed by or on behalf of the contractor, the damage to the drywall and floor covering will not be covered by the policy since these elements were installed by subcontractors and therefore were installed "on behalf of" the contractor.

Liability for damage to the merchandise within the warehouse would, of course, be covered by the policy.

5. Broad Form

Most liability insurance companies offer a so-called broad form property damage endorsement that omits from the work exclusion the words "or on behalf of". Thus, the exclusion excludes damage to "work performed by the insured" rather than damage to "work performed by or on behalf of the insured".

Same as above, but the framing is also damaged. The framing was installed by the prime contractor.

Under the broad form endorsement, not only the merchandise, but also the drywall and floor covering would be covered by the policy, while framing would not be covered since it is work performed "by the insured"

Prudent prime contractors usually purchase the broad form property damage endorsement.

6. Subcontractor's Insurance

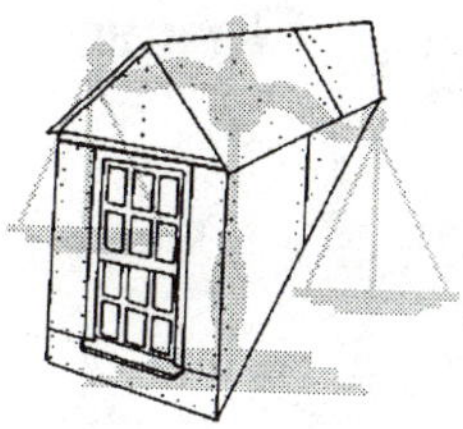

Same as above. O makes a claim against K for damage caused by water intrusion. K makes a claim against S (roofing subcontractor), seeking indemnity against K's potential liability to O. Assume that the water intrusion was caused by defective roofing work.

Here, S's commercial general liability policy would cover damage to the ceiling, drywall, floor covering, framing, and merchandise, but would not cover the cost of repairing or replacing the roof itself, since this is "work performed by the insured".

7. The Duty to Defend

A liability insurance carrier has the right and the duty to defend an insured contractor against claims for damage that fall within the coverage of the policy. This gives the insured some peace of mind, for it protects against attorneys fees and costs of litigation. The contractor, of course, has the duty to cooperate with the insurance company in establishing any legitimate defenses.

The existence of the duty to defend the insured against a claim is determined at the time when the claim is first made against the insured contractor. In order to get the greatest benefit from their insurance polices, contractors should promptly tender the defense of claims to their insurance carriers. ("Tender the defense" means to notify the carrier of the claim and call upon the carrier to defend it.)

8. Reservation of Rights

Since an insurance carrier may not know, at the time of tender, whether a claim will be covered by the policy, it may send to the insured a "reservation of rights" letter. In such a letter, the insurance carrier undertakes to defend against the claim while reserving the right to deny that the claim is covered by the policy and also reserving the right, if further investigation discloses that no claim is covered by the policy, to withdraw the defense.

9. Progressive Loss

K builds a house for O in 1997. The foundation settles gradually. In 2000, a sewer lateral breaks. Effluence from the sewer lateral gradually washes out the soil, and in 2002 the stucco walls begin to crack. O (owner), who first notices the settlement damage in 2001, files a claim with her property insurance carrier and also makes a claim of defective construction against K (contractor). O changes insurance carriers in 1999 and against in 2001.

O should present her claim to all three carriers. Insurance coverage is "triggered" by the occurrence of actual physical damage. In some states, a "continuous trigger" applies and therefore all three policies would respond to the loss. In other states, a "manifestation" trigger applies, and the policy that was in force when the damage first became manifest would cover the loss.

Now, let's look at the insurance coverage situation from K's standpoint. Assume that K had three different liability insurance policies in effect, having changed carriers also in 1999 and 2001. K should tender the defense to all three carriers. A policy or policies that will cover the loss will be determined according to whether the state courts have adopted "continuous trigger" or "manifestation trigger".

10. Efficient Cause

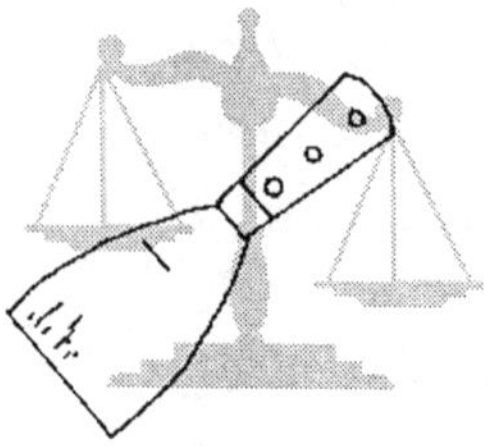

Same as above. O's property insurance policies exclude losses caused by soil settlement, soil movement, and earth movement.

Whether O's loss will be covered by her property insurance policy depends upon whether the "efficient, proximate" cause of the loss was soil settlement, or a broken sewer lateral. If the “efficient, moving, proximate” cause is determined to be the broken sewer lateral, then the loss is covered even though soil settlement also occurred.

Case in Point

Many construction contracts provide that the project owner will purchase builders risk insurance protecting the project against damage by fire and other risks, and will name the prime contractor and subcontractors as additional insureds. If an owner fails to comply with such contract requirements, in effect, the owner becomes the insurer of the prime contractor and subcontractors. In other words, the owner is required to do what the insurance company would otherwise have done. In a case that arose in Iowa, an owner who had signed a contract with such a provision failed to name subcontractors as additional insureds. The project was damaged by fire caused by negligent installation of an electrical outlet which caused a short circuit which started a fire. The owner's insurance company paid for the loss, and the owner and the insurance company filed a joint action against the electrical subcontractor who had negligently caused the fire. The court held, however, that the owner and the insurance carrier could not make out a claim against the subcontractor, because when the owner agreed to provide fire insurance naming the subcontractor as an additional insured, and failed to do so, the owner became the subcontractor's insurer. Since the owner insured the subcontractor against loss by fire, the owner could not sue the subcontractor for loss by fire. Connor v Thompson Construction & Development Co, 166 NW2d 109 (Iowa 1969).

CHAPTER 11

MECHANICS LIENS

1. Merchant
2. Mechanics Lien Claimant
3. Indemnity
4. Insolvent Contractor
5. Payment Bond
6. Blanket Waiver
7. Estoppel
8. Conditional Release
9. Joint Check
10. Preliminary Notice
11. Equitable Indemnity
12. Equitable Indemnity II
13. Equity
14. Priority
15. Mechanics Lien Priority
16. Stop Notices
17. Stop Notices on Private Projects

CHAPTER 11

MECHANICS LIENS

1. Merchant

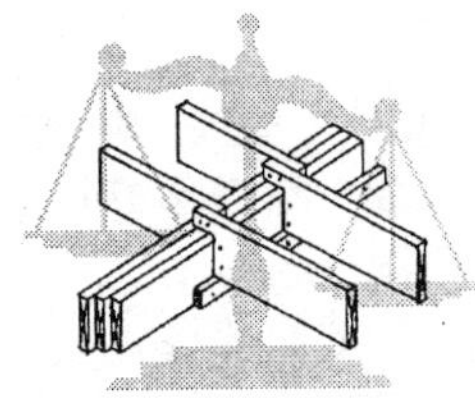

M (material supplier) sells a bookcase to R (retailer) who sells it to O (owner), who pays cash for it. R fails to pay M, who then sues O for the price of the bookcase.

Judgment for O. Although the material supplied by M may have benefited O, O has no contract with M and no obligation to pay M. The law regards M as simply suffering the consequences of bad business judgment in advancing credit to R. Moreover, to require O to pay R's debt to M would be to require O to pay for the same bookcase twice.

2. Mechanics Lien Claimant

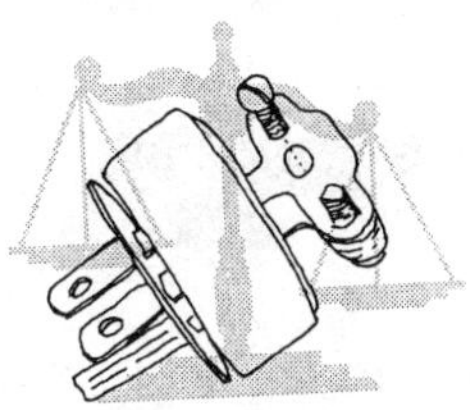

Same as above, except M is a supplier of hardwood to K (contractor) who uses the hardwood to construct a built-in bookcase for O.

Judgment for M against O. M has the right to foreclose a claim of mechanics lien against O's property, and if O doesn't pay the judgment, the property will be sold by the sheriff to the highest bidder at public auction, and the proceeds of the auction will be used to pay K's debt to M.

Legal Lore

Mechanics lien laws have been enacted in all 50 states. The purpose of the mechanics lien law is to encourage commerce by providing a form of security that contractors and suppliers who contribute to construction projects will be paid for their work and materials. In some instances the enforcement of a mechanics lien will prevent the unjust enrichment of a property owner at the expense of a contractor or material supplier. In other instances, however, as in the above example, the owner may have to "pay twice".

3. Indemnity

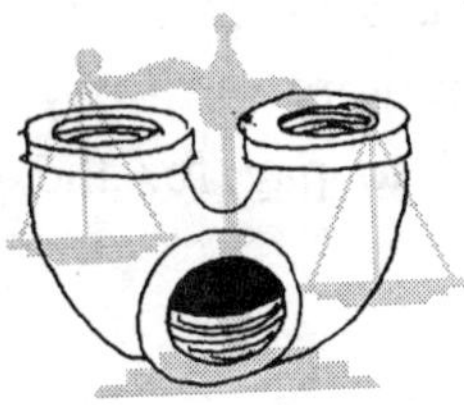

Same as above. O pays the lien and sues K for indemnity.

Judgment for O. A contractor is legally obliged to protect a property owner against mechanics lien claims.

4. Insolvent Contractor

Same as above, but K takes bankruptcy.

Here, O is precluded by K's insolvency from recovering indemnity for the cost of paying off the mechanics lien claim.

5. Payment Bond

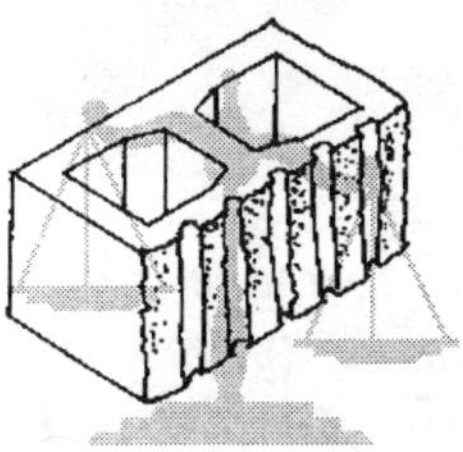

Same as above, but O, at the time of contracting, required K to furnish a payment bond. O demands that the surety on the payment bond pay off the lien.

O is protected. The principal (contractor) and surety (bonding company) on the payment bond guarantee that K will pay off all valid mechanics lien claims.

Business Pointer

It is the prime contractor's obligation to protect the owner's property against mechanics lien claims. By requiring the contractor to supply a payment bond, a property owner may obtain protection against any unwillingness, or inability (through insolvency) of the prime contractor to fulfill that

duty. The premiums for payment bonds run about $10 per $1,000 of coverage. There is also a "substandard" bond market in which premiums run considerably higher.

6. Blanket Waiver

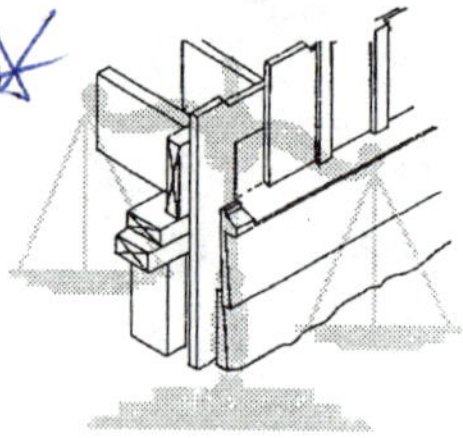

K (contractor) requires S (subcontractor) to sign a subcontract form under which S waives all mechanics lien rights.

In most states, blanket advance waivers of mechanics lien rights are void.

7. Estoppel

O (owner) refuses to make a progress payment to K (prime contractor) until K supplies mechanics lien release forms signed by all subcontractors and suppliers. In order to induce S (subcontractor) to sign a release, K promises prompt payment. S, trusting K, signs the release and delivers it to K, who delivers it to O. O, relying on the release, issues a progress payment to K. K uses the progress payment to buy a race horse, and doesn't pay S. S cancels the release for failure of consideration and records a mechanics lien against O's property. O sets up the release as a defense.

Judgment for O. O relied on the release when it made the progress payment to K. Therefore S is not permitted to cancel the release.

Legalese. *Under the legal doctrine of estoppel, a person who has lead another to believe that certain facts are true, is estopped to falsify those facts after the other person has relied upon the truth of those facts to the other person's detriment. Here, O relied upon the validity of the release when it made payment to K and therefore S is estopped to deny the validity of the release.*

---

8. Conditional Release

Same as above, but the release signed by S provides that its effectiveness is conditional upon receipt of payment.

Here, the release is ineffective because the condition (payment to S) has not been fulfilled, and O could not rely on the release because the condition was written on the face of the release.

9. Joint Check

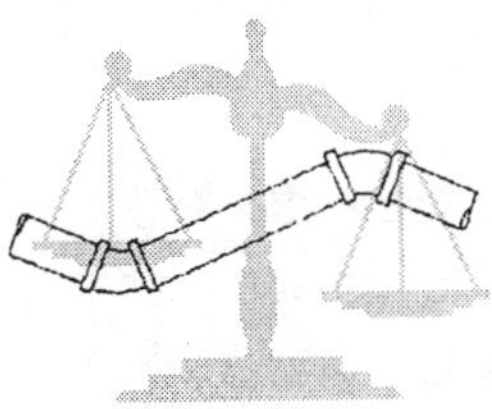

Same as above (M signs a conditional release). The conditional release signed by M provides that its effectiveness is conditioned upon payment of $10,000. K presents the form of

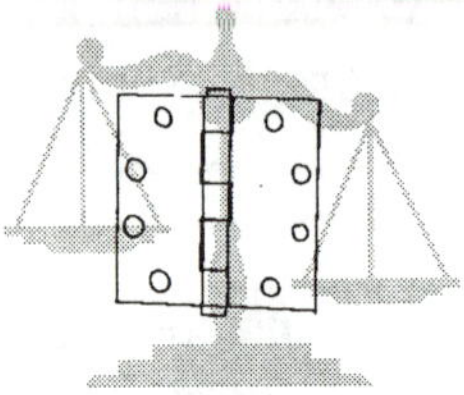

release to O, who issues a check for $10,000 payable jointly to K, S, and M. M endorses the check and hands it to S, and S hands to M its check for $10,000. S's check bounces. M records a claim of lien. O sets up the conditional release as a defense.

Judgment for O. The condition was fulfilled when M endorsed the check, even though S's check bounced. By endorsing the check, M lead O to believe that it had been paid, and is estopped to deny the fact of payment.

Business Pointer

For better protection, O should print the following legend on its checks:

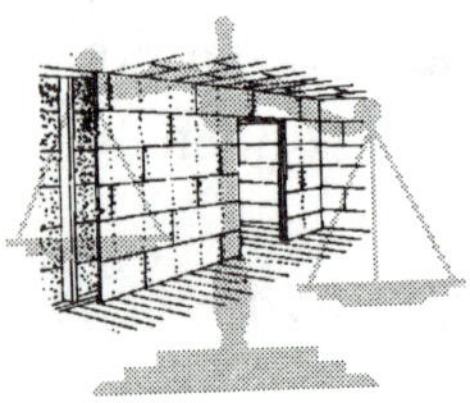

Each endorser acknowledges payment of the full face amount of this check.

Some owners prefer to avoid issuing joint checks by writing direct checks to potential lien claimants who have issued conditional releases. An owner who makes direct payment to subcontractors and suppliers should obtain the written consent of the prime contractor to apply the amount of the direct payment to the prime contract price.

10. Preliminary Notice

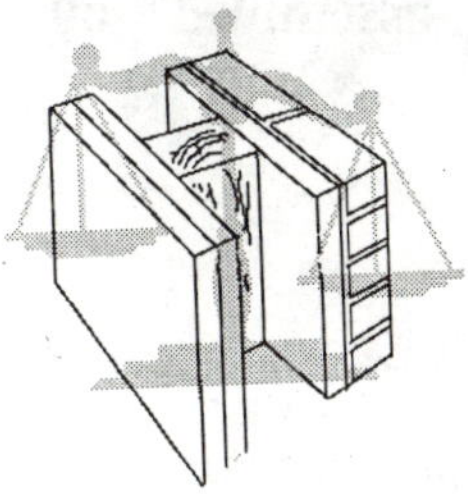

State law requires that a mechanics lien claimant who is not employed directly by the project owner must give an early preliminary notice, in writing, to the project owner to preserve mechanics lien rights. M (material supplier) employed by S (subcontractor) fails to give the notice. M proves that even though O (owner) did not receive a preliminary notice O was aware of the fact that M was supplying materials to the project.

Here, M would lose its lien rights for failure to give the preliminary notice. The purpose of the preliminary notice is to enable O to protect itself against mechanics lien claims. Therefore actual notice is no substitute for the required written preliminary notice, since O is entitled to assume that if M did not give a preliminary notice M did not intend to preserve its mechanics lien rights.

Business Pointer

A property owner may protect itself against mechanics lien claims by requiring the prime contractor to supply valid releases from all

subcontractors and suppliers who may have established mechanics lien rights. The prudent owner makes no payment to the prime contractor until the prime contractor has assembled all necessary releases.

11. Equitable Indemnity

M (material supplier), unpaid by S (subcontractor), forecloses a mechanics lien against property belonging to O (owner). O pays off the lien and sues K (prime contractor) for indemnity.

Judgment for O. The prime contractor is obliged to protect the owner's property against mechanics lien claims.

12. Equitable Indemnity II

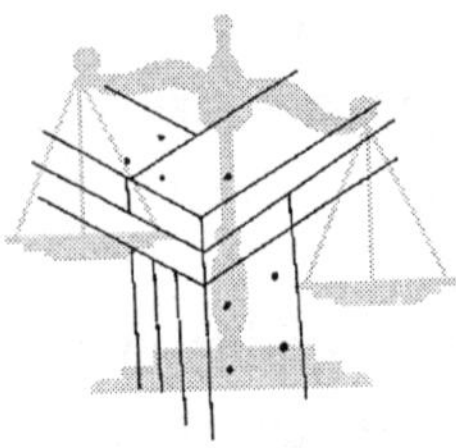

Same as above, K (prime contractor) sues S (subcontractor) for indemnity.

Judgment for K. At this point, the debt has finally been imposed on the party with the ultimate responsibility, the subcontractor who failed to pay the material supplier's bill.

13. Equity

O (owner) owns a lot subject to a $20,000 mortgage. She takes a $100,000 construction loan from a bank that is secured by a mortgage on the same lot. The proceeds of the construction loan are used to build a house on the lot. The appraised value of the improved property is $110,000.

A mechanics lien claim against such a property would be worthless because a mechanics lien only applies to the owner's equity in the property. The owner's equity is figured by subtracting from the value of the property the amounts of any mortgages. Here, the value of the property is $110,000 and the amount of the combined mortgages is $120,000, yielding a *negative* equity of $10,000.

Legal Lore

A claimant collects the value of a mechanics lien claim when the sheriff, acting on a writ issued by a judge, sells the owner's interest in the property at public auction. If the property is worth less than the encumbrances against it, the auction will attract no bids and the sheriff will never get the money to pay off the mechanics lien claim.

14. Priority

A mechanics lien claim, like a mortgage, is a form of security for the payment of a debt. If the debt is not paid, the creditor can sell the security and use the proceeds of the sale to pay off the debt. Security interests in real estate are ranked according to priority. Interests holding higher priority are paid off 100% before interests of lower priority receive anything.

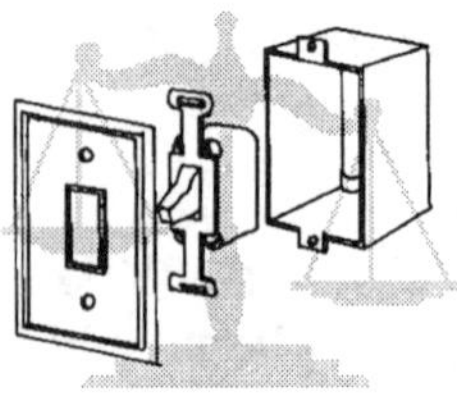

Property worth $110,000 is encumbered by a first mortgage of $100,000 and a second mortgage of $20,000. The mortgages go into default and are foreclosed. The sale produces $110,000.

Here, the entire proceeds of the sale are paid to the holder of the first mortgage, and the holder of the second mortgage gets nothing. Such a worthless second mortgage is known as a "sold out second".

15. Mechanics Lien Priority

In many states a mechanics lien takes its priority from the date when construction first commences on the overall project. This puts mechanics lien claimants in competition for priority with the financial institutions that make construction loans.

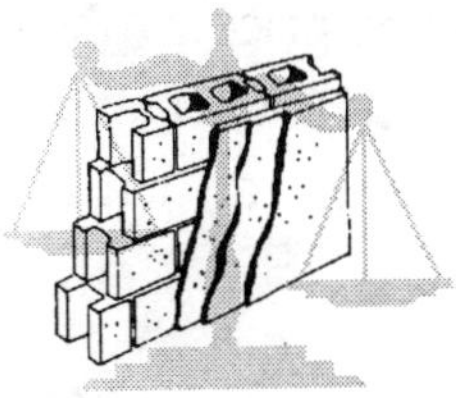

S (subcontractor) starts digging for footings on January 1. Mortgage securing a construction loan records on January 10. P (painter) paints the project in October. He records a claim of mechanics lien in December.

Here, P's mechanics lien claim would take priority over the mortgage securing the construction loan. In foreclosure, the sheriff would pay 100% of P's claim before paying anything to the financial institution holding the mortgage.

In other states, mechanics lien claims take priority as of the date when the claimant first started work on the project, or as of the date when the claim is filed or recorded.

16. Stop Notices

Mechanics liens are not allowed on public projects. It would be unworkable for an unpaid subcontractor to become the owner of a police station or a city hall by foreclosure of a mechanics lien.

As a substitute for the mechanics lien remedy, the legislatures in most states have provided the stop notice. A stop notice applies not to real property, but to construction funds.

When a public agency undertakes a public project, it establishes a construction budget. The agency commits a sum of money equivalent to the contract price to the construction of the project. It is this money, rather than the real property on which the project is located, that is subject to stop notices.

The stop notice right is enforced by the unpaid claimant giving notice to the public agency of its claim. The agency is then required to set aside a sufficient sum of money to answer the claim. In effect, the stop notice interrupts the flow of construction money from the agency to the prime contractor.

The end result of the enforcement of a stop notice is entry of a judgment in favor of the claimant and against the public agency for the amount of the claim.

17. Stop Notices on Private Projects

In some states, the stop notice remedy has been extended to private projects as well as public projects. In these states, the remedy applies not only to construction funds in the hands of the project owner, but also to construction funds committed to the project by a financial institution in the form of proceeds of a construction loan. As in the case of public projects, the end result of the enforcement of a stop notice is entry of a judgment in favor of the claimant and against the project owner (or the construction lender) for the amount of the claim.

The mechanics lien and the stop notice are considered to be concurrent remedies. This means that a claimant may choose to enforce its mechanics lien rights, or its stop notice rights, or both at the same time. Many claimants consider the stop notice to be a more effective remedy than the mechanics lien claim, since it applies leverage by interrupting the flow of funds to the developer or prime contractor.

Case in Point

The basic function of a mechanics lien is to prevent an owner from being unjustly enriched at the expense of a contractor or a material supplier. It is for this reason that the amount of a mechanics lien is generally limited to the reasonable value of the work or materials supplied to a project. But what about a situation in which a contractor makes a claim against a project owner because the owner interfered with the contractor's operation and thereby made the construction of the project more expensive than the contractor had anticipated? This gives the contractor a claim against the owner, all right, but is the claim secured by mechanics lien rights? According to a California court decision, the answer is no: A contractor's claim against the owner for damages for delay is not secured by mechanics lien rights. Lambert v Superior Court, 228 Cal App 3d 383 (1991).

CHAPTER 12

BONDS AND BONDING

1. Principal and Surety
2. Release Bond
3. Payment Bond
4. Indemnity on Bond
5. Indemnity from Subcontractor
6. Performance Bonds

CHAPTER 12

BONDS AND BONDING

1. Principal and Surety

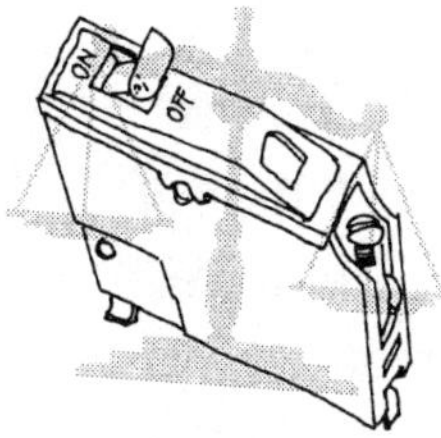

D borrows $1,000 from the bank and M, her mother, guarantees that D will repay the loan.

S is "principal," M is "surety," and the bank is "obligee." Suretyship is a legal relationship between three parties in which one party guarantees to another that the third party will perform an obligation.

2. Release Bond

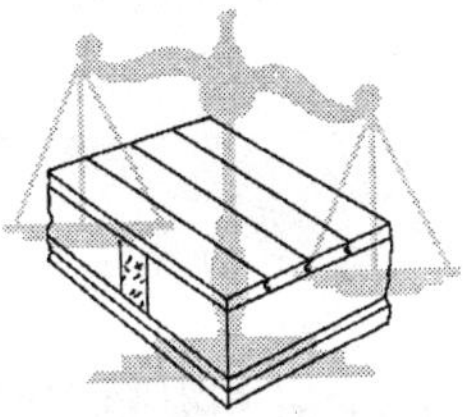

C (claimant) records a claim of mechanics lien against property belonging to O (owner). O obtains a release bond, records it, and sends a copy to C.

The recording of the release bond removes the claim of lien from the title to the property. Now, if C establishes that its lien was valid, it will recover the amount of its claim from the bonding company.

Business Pointer

Although the premium on the bond may be relatively modest (in the neighborhood of 1% per annum) the bonding company will usually demand collateral before it will be willing to write the bond. Assume, for example, that the mechanics lien law requires that the release bond be 125% of the mechanics lien claim.

If the lien is $100,000, the amount of the release bond will be $125,000. The annual premium will be $1,250. Before it would write the bond, however, the surety might demand collateral worth $125,000. An example of collateral would be a real estate mortgage, or a certificate of deposit, or a cash deposit of $125,000. The purpose of the collateral is to protect the bonding company against loss in defending against, and potentially paying off, the lien claim. This, from an immediate cash flow point of view, it could cost an owner more to "bond a lien" than to pay it off.

3. Payment Bond

K (contractor) signs a contract with O (owner) to build a warehouse. As required by the contract, K supplies a payment bond to protect the project against mechanics lien claims.

Business Pointer

It is a prime contractor's obligation to protect an owner's property against mechanics liens. Many prudent owners require prime contractors to furnish a payment bond (sometimes called a labor and material bond) to guarantee the performance of that obligation. The contractor is the principal on the payment bond.

In most states, a payment bond is combined with a performance bond at no additional premium. (The premium for such a combined bond runs about $10 per $1,000.) The contractor pays the premium and the amount of the premium is, of course, added to the contract price so it is paid, in the end, by the owner.

Unlike the release bond discussed above, a payment bond does not remove a mechanics lien claim from the title to property. A payment bond is, however, a source of recovery for a mechanics lien claimant as well as a protection, for the owner, against mechanics lien claims.

4. Indemnity on Bond

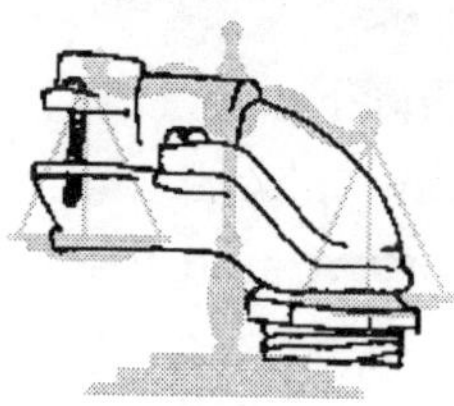

M (material supplier), unpaid by S (subcontractor), records a claim of mechanics lien against property owned by O (owner). M files suit against S for breach of contract and against O to foreclose the

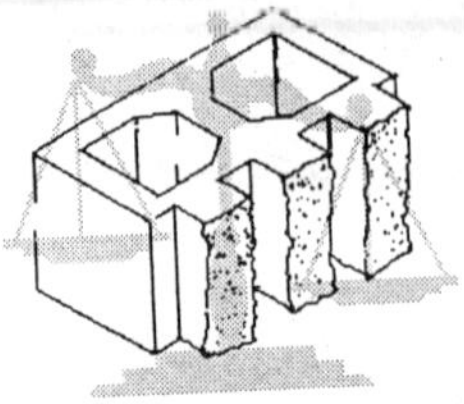

mechanics lien claim. In the same action O sues K (prime contractor) and B (bonding company) as the principal and surety on the payment bond that was provided by K for the protection of O. B demands indemnity from K.

1) M has a direct right of action against K and B on the bond.

2) M may join its action on the bond with its action against S (to collect its bill for materials purchased by S) and O (for foreclosure of mechanics lien).

3) The principal on a bond (here, K) is obliged to defend and indemnify the surety (here, B) against claims arising under the bond.

5. Indemnity from Subcontractor

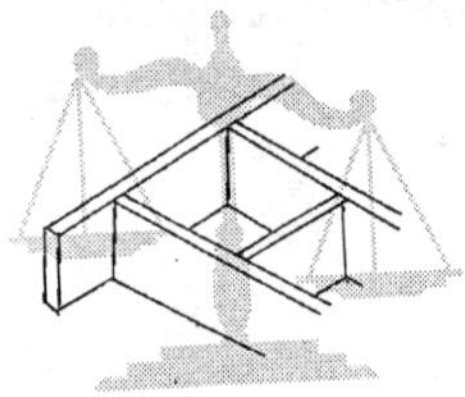

K (prime contractor) files a cross-complaint against S (subcontractor) for indemnity against M's (material supplier's) claim.

K is entitled to indemnity from S. Under a concept known as "equitable indemnity" the law places the ultimate burden of a claim on the most responsible party. Here, the most responsible party is S, because the whole problem originated with the fact that S failed to pay its debt to M.

Unfortunately for K, S may be insolvent and unable to pay its debt. For this reason, prime contractors sometimes require performance and payment bonds from their subcontractors.

6. Performance Bonds

A performance bond is an instrument under which a bonding company (surety) guarantees that a contractor (the principal) will perform its contracts. This guarantee is usually made to the project owner (obligee) although occasionally the guarantee may also be for the benefit of a construction lender.

The premium for a performance bond is relatively modest (on the order of 1% of the amount of the bond). Before a bonding company will issue a performance bond it will usually make a thorough investigation of the experience, ability, and financial strength of the contractor. Bonding companies usually require that the principal officers of a contractor sign agreements under which they agree to hold the bonding company harmless against any loss on the bond. Thus, the principal officers of the contractor become "indemnitors".

In most states, performance and payment bonds are required for all public contracts. Private owners, however, seldom require bonds of their contractors, partly to save the bond premium and partly because they are willing to deal with contractors who do not have "bonding capacity." (A contractor does not have bonding capacity when, because of inadequate experience or financial strength, it is unable to obtain bonding.)

Case in Point

A surety who guarantees that a contractor will perform a construction contract is not liable for losses that the owner brings upon itself. In a construction contract, the contractor agrees to perform a construction project for the benefit of the owner in return for payment of the contract price by the owner to the contractor. The primary, in fact, usually the only, motivation for the contractor to perform the contract is payment. For this reason, most construction contracts are performed under a progress payment system since the owner realizes that if he paid the contractor up front, the contractor would be lacking in motivation to finish the job. In recognition of this situation, many courts hold that prepayment exonerates a performance bond. In an early California case, the contractor agreed to build a high school for $5,580. (In those days, a dollar was worth a dollar.) The contract price was to be paid in three installments of $1,860 each. The first payment was to be made when all building materials had been delivered to the site. When the contractor had delivered no more than the rough lumber, it applied for and received its first payment, pocketed the money, abandoned the contract, and left the lumber on the site without paying for it. The California Supreme Court held that the bond was exonerated by prepayment, since the reward for further performance was lost and the temptation to act dishonestly was increased. Glenn County v Jones, 146 Cal 518 (1905).

CHAPTER 13

STATUTES OF LIMITATIONS

1. **Limitation on Written Contract**
2. **Limitation on Oral Contract**
3. **Accrual of Cause of Action**
4. **Limitation Changed by Contract**
5. **Construction Defect**
6. **Statute of Repose**

CHAPTER 13

STATUTES OF LIMITATIONS

1. Limitation on Written Contract

Under a written contract, K builds a garage for O but O refuses to pay for the work. Five years later, K sues O for the payment.

Judgment for O. The statute of limitations for filing an action for breach of a written contract is four years.

2. Limitation on Oral Contract

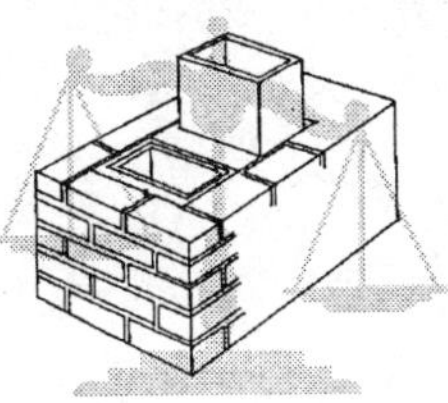

The contract is oral, and K waits three years to sue.

Judgment for O again. The statute of limitations for an action for breach of an oral contract is two years.

Note. Limitations periods vary from state to state.

3. Accrual of Cause of Action

K sues two years after the breach, which is two years and six months after the contract was formed.

The statutory period runs from the time when the cause of action arose, which means the time when K first had the right to sue O. Here, the statute did not expire because K sued within two years of the breach.

4. Limitation Changed by Contract

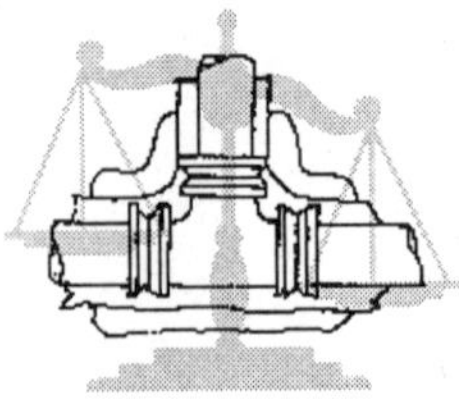

The written contract between O and K provides that any action by one party against the other must be filed within one year after the completion of the project.

This changes the limitations period from four years to one year. It also changes the rule that the statute of limitations only begins to run when a cause of action arises.

5. Construction Defect

Five years after its completion, an apartment complex begins to settle because of improperly compacted fill.

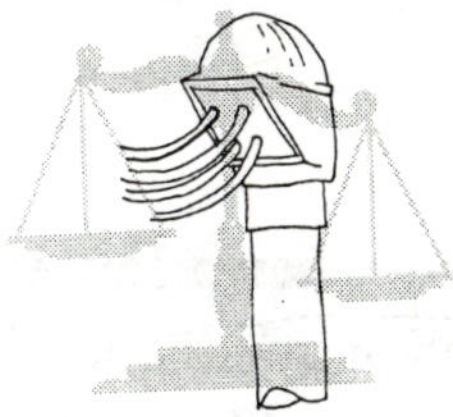

After attempting to negotiate a settlement, O sues K for breach of contract six years after the completion of the project and one year after O discovered the breach.

The suit is timely. The statute of limitations runs from accrual of a cause of action, and the cause of action arose when O discovered that the fill was improperly compacted.

6. Statute of Repose

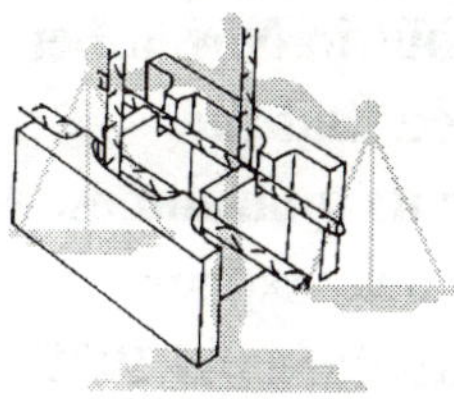

The settlement occurred and the improper compaction was discovered ten years after completion of the project, and O files suit against K one year later.

In most states, K is protected by a "statute of repose" that eliminates causes of action for construction defects ten years after the completion of a project.

Legalese. *A statute of repose is a measure adopted by a state legislature to protect architects, engineers, builders, and contractors against liability unlimited in time. A cause of action cannot accrue more than ten years after the completion of a project because the legislature has decreed that such a cause of action does not exist. (The period varies in different states between 7 and 15 years.)*

Case in Point

The statute of limitations starts to run when a cause of action arises. When a cause of action arises out of a construction defect, it may arise a considerable period of time after the completion of the project. For example, in the case of a church project that was completed in the late 70's, a roofing manufacturer guaranteed that the roof would be maintained in a watertight condition provided owner would give contractor notice of leaks within 30 days of discovery. Leaks were repaired in 1980 and again in 1982. More leaks occurred in 1984 but in November of 1986 the owner was informed that the manufacturer was refusing to honor its guarantees. The owner replaced the roofs at its own expense in 1987 and filed suit against the manufacturer in 1989. The owner obtained a judgment for $358,613.54 in spite of the fact that suit was filed more than seven years after the project had been completed. The court held that the four-year statute of limitations did not bar the action since the breach did not occur until November 1986 when the owner was informed that the manufacturer would not honor the guarantee. Church of the Nativity of Our Lord v Watpro, Inc, 491 NW2d 1 (Minn 1992).

CHAPTER 14
ARBITRATION

CHAPTER 14

ARBITRATION

1. Arbitration Agreement

In early law, arbitration agreements were not enforceable. Congress changed that when it adopted the Federal Arbitration Act in 1925. Since then, almost every state has passed an arbitration law under which arbitration agreements and awards are enforced. Acting under these arbitration laws, courts encourage parties to resolve commercial disputes by binding private arbitration.

Architect and owner sign an AIA form contract for architectural services that includes an arbitration clause. The owner sues the architect for malpractice. The architect demands arbitration.

Here, if the owner does not voluntarily participate in the arbitration proceedings, the court will postpone the lawsuit pending arbitration, and order the owner to arbitrate.

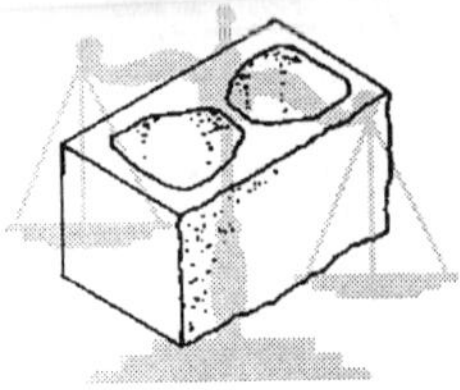

Acting under the arbitration clause, the American Arbitration Association appoints an arbitrator and a hearing is scheduled. The owner boycotts the hearing. The arbitrator signs an award based on evidence introduced at the hearing by the architect.

The award is enforceable.

2. Enforcement of Award

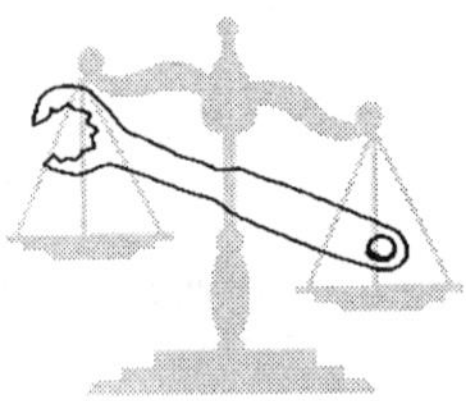

After hearings, an arbitrator issues an award requiring a project owner to pay a specified sum of money to a contractor. The owner refuses to pay.

The contractor in such a case may file a petition requesting that the court confirm the award. Once it is confirmed, the award is enforced as a judgment of the court.

3. Neutrality of Arbitrator

In order to be able to make an award that will stand up in court, an arbitrator must be *neutral*. An arbitrator must disclose any relationship with the parties to a dispute, or their counsel or witnesses, if knowledge of the relationship would cause a reasonable person to believe that the arbitrator would be biased in favor of, or against, one of the parties. The parties may waive objection. In the absence of such a waiver, the arbitrator will resign or, if the arbitrator refuses to resign, will be removed by court order.

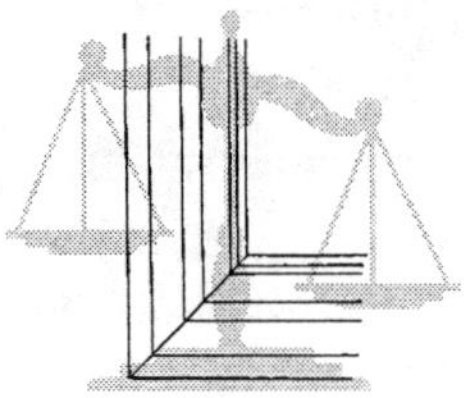

In an arbitration between an owner and a contractor, the arbitrator discloses that she was once employed as an attorney by a company that is related to the owner. The contractor makes no objection, and the hearings proceed. The arbitrator makes an award in favor of the owner. The contractor files a motion in court seeking to vacate the award.

Here, the contractor waived any objection by continuing with the hearings after the arbitrator disclosed her potential bias. A party may not speculate on the outcome of an arbitration proceeding and then object to the jurisdiction of the arbitrator only after learning the outcome.

4. Selection of the Arbitrator

Parties often jointly select an arbitrator. Lists of qualified arbitrators are available in a number of commercially published directories, and from dispute resolution services such as the American Arbitration Association.

Many construction industry arbitrations are handled under the rules of the American Arbitration

Association, which is designated in arbitration clauses contained in the AIA documents and many other standard forms.

Under the AAA rules, the AAA furnishes to the parties a list of qualified arbitrators from which the parties may cross off any unacceptable names and then rank in order of preference the remaining names. The AAA then appoints the arbitrator according to preferences expressed by the parties.

Construction industry disputes are usually arbitrated by lawyers who specialize in the field of construction law or by retired judges who have had construction industry experience. For the larger cases, arbitration is by a panel of three arbitrators: usually a lawyer, a contractor, and an architect or engineer.

One popular method of arbitration calls for each party to designate an arbitrator and for the two "partisan" arbitrators to select the third, "neutral" arbitrator. The partisan arbitrators are expected to represent the points of view of the opposing parties. The award is made by any two arbitrators.

5. The Award

In most states, arbitrators can make any award that a judge could make.

The award must be based on evidence and arguments submitted by the parties at hearings. Construction industry awards are usually for a sum of money to be paid by one party to the other. The arbitrator may award the expenses of arbitration to the prevailing party. If the contract between the parties has an attorneys fees clause, an arbitrator will also award attorneys fees to the winning party.

6. Attack on Award

Arbitration awards are considered "more final" than court judgments, since court judgments are subject to appeal and reversal if the trial judge made an error in law. It is almost impossible to successfully attack an arbitration award. Arbitration awards will not normally be vacated on the ground that an arbitrator made a mistake in law. Arbitrators, who are not necessarily lawyers, do not necessarily know the law, and may make awards based on their ideas of justice, equity, and trade practice.

An arbitration award may, however, be vacated for fraud or corruption of the arbitrators or for the failure of the arbitrators to give a fair hearing.

A fair hearing is a hearing of which parties have adequate notice, and where parties are allowed to present their evidence and to cross examine the witnesses presented by the opposing party.

7. Multiple Party Arbitration

O (owner) employs K (contractor) to remodel a home. K employs S (subcontractor) to install a new roof. The roof leaks. O demands arbitration against S.

O has no contract with S and therefore no right to require S to arbitrate the dispute.

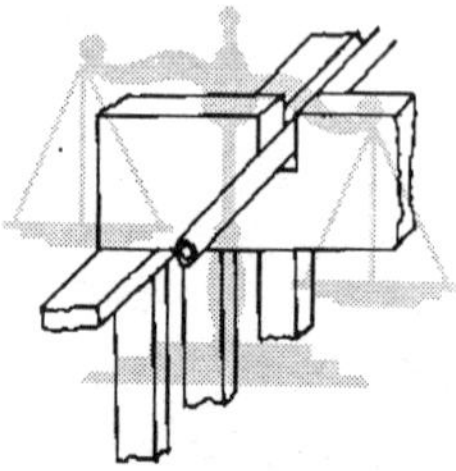

Same as above. The arbitration clause in the contract between O and K provides that all subcontractors are bound to participate in any arbitration of disputes arising out of the construction of the project.

Same result, S is not a party to the contract between O and K.

Same as above, but the form of subcontract between K and S incorporates the terms of the prime contract into the subcontract.

Here, S is bound to arbitrate, since it signed a document that incorporated the arbitration clause.

8. Bias of Arbitrator

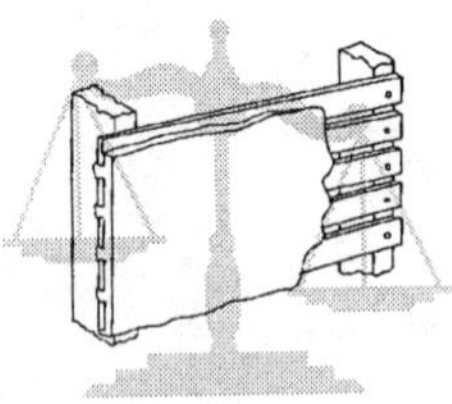

O (owner) and K (contractor) submit to arbitration a dispute in which O claims that S (subcontractor), a roofer employed by K, installed a defective roof that leaks.

Here K is responsible for the roof even though it was installed by a subcontractor. Prime contractors are responsible for work installed by their subcontractors.

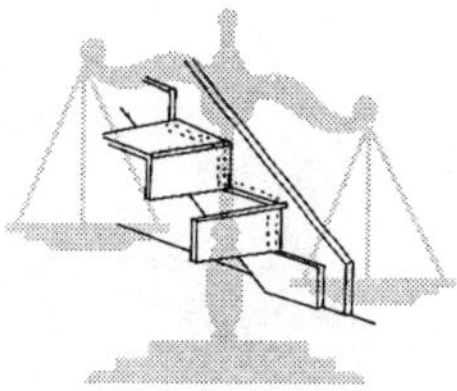

Same as above. A (arbitrator) finds that the roof is not defective and enters an award in favor of K. O then learns that A is a member of a law firm that has performed legal services for S.

In such a case, a court would vacate the award. Since A's law firm has represented S as a client, it would be presumed that A would be biased in favor of S and would be reluctant to enter an award against a client of the law firm.

An arbitration award will be vacated if a reasonable person would believe that it resulted from possible bias of the arbitrator in favor of or against one of the parties to the arbitration proceeding. Arbitrators and potential arbitrators must be careful to disclose to the parties any relationships that might create an impression of possible bias. The parties, in turn, may waive objection after an arbitrator makes such a disclosure. If objection is not waived, a new arbitrator must be appointed.

9. Selection of the Arbitrator

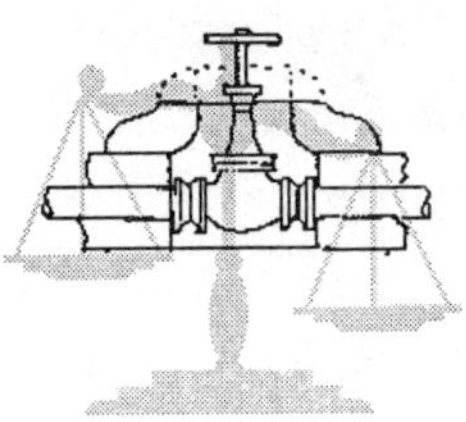

An arbitration clause in a contract between K (contractor) and O (owner) provides that in the event of a dispute K and O will each appoint an arbitrator and the two arbitrators so

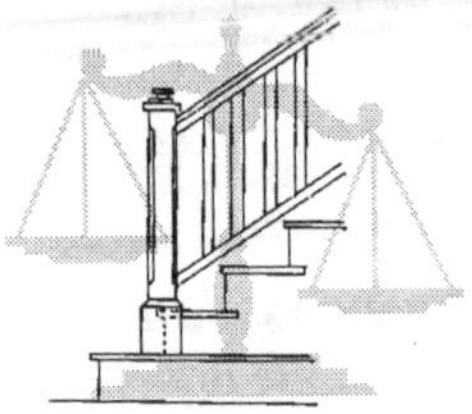

selected will appoint a third arbitrator, the award to be signed by any two arbitrators. A dispute arises, K and O appoint their arbitrators, but the two arbitrators can't agree as to the selection of the third arbitrator.

In the case of such an impasse, a court will appoint the third arbitrator.

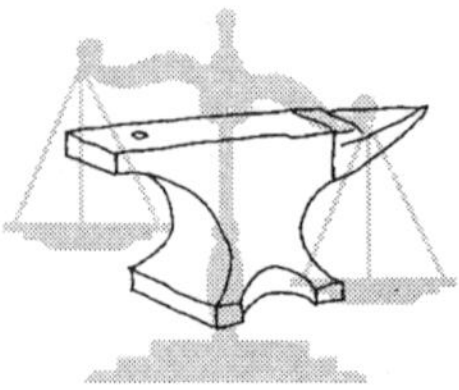

O objects that the arbitrator appointed by K is a licensed contractor, and therefore is likely to be biased in favor of K.

An arbitrator appointed by a party is expected to represent the position of the party who made the appointment. The ultimate award is expected to be made by the third "neutral" arbitrator joined by one of the "partisan" arbitrators.

10. Rules of Evidence

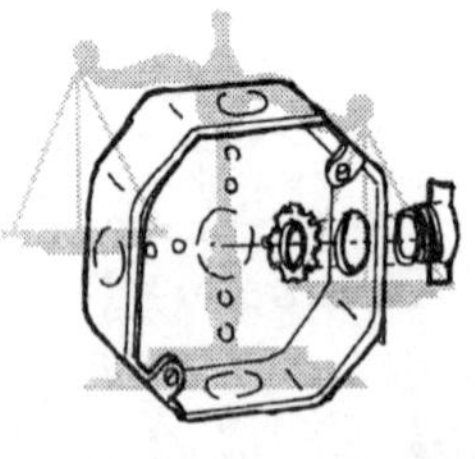

At an arbitration hearing, a party objects to the introduction of a contract into evidence on the ground that the document is a copy, rather than original, and therefore violates the "best evidence" rule. The arbitrator overrules the objection.

Arbitrators are not required to follow rules of evidence, and may rule on objections based upon their own judgment as to the reliability of exhibits and testimony offered by the parties.

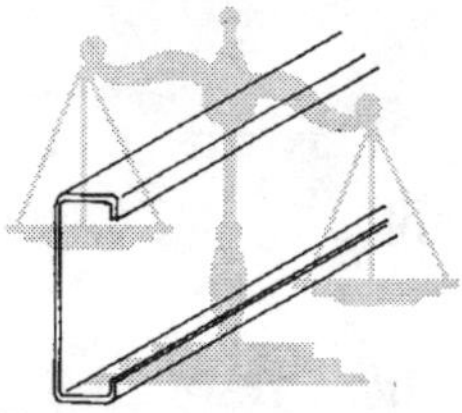

A party objects to testimony offered in an arbitration proceeding on the ground that the testimony sought to be introduced is covered by the attorney client privilege.

Arbitrators are required to respect privileges, including the attorney-client privilege and the privilege against self incrimination.

11. Sham Arbitration Agreement

W (worker) finds a "receipt for employee handbook" which contains an agreement that any disputes between W and E (employer) will be finally resolved by binding arbitration as provided in the handbook. The handbook requires disputes to be arbitrated by a committee of five composed of two employees, two managers, and the general manager. Tie votes will be broken by the general manager. The committee is required to resolve disputes in accordance with policies

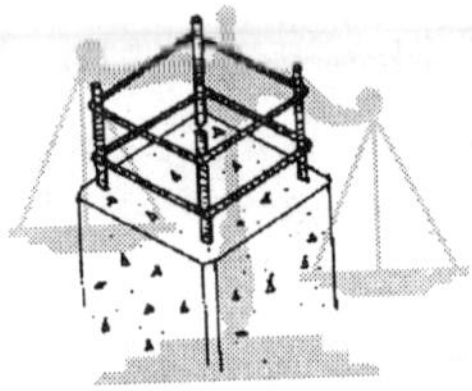

established by the company. W files a lawsuit against E seeking damages for wrongful termination. E files a petition to compel arbitration.

The court would deny the petition. It is true that arbitration agreements are enforceable, but this agreement is not an arbitration agreement. "Arbitration" is defined as a dispute resolution procedure where the parties to the dispute have a right to present evidence at a hearing before an *impartial* arbitrator to make a final and binding decision. Here, the arbitrator is not impartial because it is composed of employees and managers who are within the control of the company. The public policy favoring arbitration as a means of dispute resolution would be undermined if the courts were to enforce unfair and overreaching agreements that put one party at the mercy of the other.

Case in Point

The courts encourage arbitration and therefore parties usually enforce arbitration agreements. Courts also recognize that arbitration would get a bad name if it came to be viewed as a biased system that could be used to deprive parties of a fair hearing. Therefore the courts are reluctant to enforce an arbitration agreement that doesn't provide for a fair hearing. In a California case, an employee filed suit against a hotel company for wrongful termination, and the hotel company demanded that the case be arbitrated under an arbitration clause in the employee handbook that the employee had signed off on when she had first been employed. Under the arbitration proceedings established in the employee handbook, claims of employees would be decided by a review committee composed of two hotel employees and two hotel managers and the general manager of the hotel. In the case of a tie, the general manager was to cast the deciding vote. Under the rules, the review committee was required to decide all disputes in accordance with hotel policy. The court held that the employee was not bound by the arbitration clause because it was fundamentally unfair, since the arbitrator was not neutral. Since all the members of the review committee were either employees or managers of the hotel, the review committee was subject to control by the hotel and therefore the dispute resolution system established by the contract was not an arbitration

system entitled to enforcement by the courts. Arbitration requires that the decision be made by a neutral arbitrator, and the courts will not enforce arbitration agreements that are inherently biased against one of the parties. Cheng-Canindin v Renaissance Hotel Associates, 50 Cal App 4th 676 (1996).

CHAPTER 15

AFFIRMATIVE ACTION AND PREVAILING WAGES

1. The Programs

2. Affirmative Action

3. Outreach Programs

4. Minorities vs. Women: Do the Same Concepts Apply?

5. Prevailing Wages

CHAPTER 15

AFFIRMATIVE ACTION AND PREVAILING WAGES

1. The Programs

We deal in this chapter with two regulatory programs that have little impact on contractors who do private work, but can have a big effect on public works contractors: affirmative action and prevailing wages. The objectives of these programs are admirable: even noble. The way they work out in administrative and political practice, however, is another thing.

The purposes behind prevailing wage laws are to avoid government benefiting from the oppression of workers who receive substandard wages and to secure for public works the benefits of a strong, skilled, and healthy labor force. The objective of affirmative action is to overcome the effect of racial and sexual discrimination and to bring to public contracting diverse skills that might otherwise be lost. In some states disabled veterans are also targeted for affirmative action.

While the governmental objectives are laudable, the political objectives have been criticized. The main political support for prevailing wages comes from union labor and union contractors seeking to avoid competition from non-union (often minority) workers and contractors.

Strong political support for affirmative action comes from those who seek racial and sexual preferences and seek to avoid competition from white males. As with all government programs that seek to closely regulate the marketplace, affirmative action and prevailing wage programs are subject to bureaucratic abuse.

2. Affirmative Action

Affirmative action programs have been passed by the federal government and by states, cities, counties, and countless commissions, districts, and local agencies. The programs can be divided into two types: quota programs and outreach programs.

Quota programs require that a public works contract bidder provide evidence that specified quotas of the work will be awarded to businesses owned by minorities or women. Outreach programs require a bidder to demonstrate good faith efforts to obtain participation by minority and women owned businesses to attempt to meet participation goals (rather than quotas) established by the public agency.

In 1995, the United States Supreme Court ruled that racial quotas may not be required of public contractors unless an agency has evidence of past discrimination and unless the program is narrowly tailored to repair the effects of past discrimination. Such programs will be subject to strict scrutiny by the courts under the Equal Protection Clause of United States Constitution. Only specific evidence of racial injustice and "narrow tailoring" of a plan to overcome its effects will justify discrimination against white males in public contracting.

Since the Supreme Court decision, a number of local agencies have abandoned quota programs until they can perform the necessary studies to justify a more narrowly tailored approach to affirmative action. Many affirmative action programs have been tested in court by bidders who contend a contract should have been awarded to them, but was not because of an affirmative action program that does not meet the requirements established by the Supreme Court. In such cases, courts may order an agency to award the contract to the low bidder rather than a bidder who meets the affirmative action requirements of the agency.

A low bidder may also sue the agency for damages. In some states damages may include profits that the bidder would have made if the contract had been awarded to the low bidder, but in other states the damages that the contractor can recover are limited to the cost of preparing the bid.

3. Outreach Programs

Many agencies have established outreach programs under which the agency establishes goals for participation by minority and women owned businesses in public contracting. The agency may then require that bidders supply evidence that they have made strenuous good faith efforts to encourage participation by minority and women owned subcontractors and suppliers. Many programs establish criteria for judging whether a bidder has made good faith efforts to attract minority and women owned businesses, among them:

- Helping MBE's and WBE's obtain insurance and bonding capacity

- Advertising for bids in minority and women owned publications

- Cooperating with minority and women oriented associations in soliciting bids

- Soliciting bids from MBE's and WBE's by direct mail

- Following up direct mail solicitations by telephone calls to encourage to MBE's and WBE's to submit bids

- Breaking a project up into small increments of work that can be performed more readily by MBE's and WBE's

- Supplying MBE's and WBE's with bidding documents, drawings, specifications, and other information to assist them in submitting bids

- Awarding work to MBE's and WBE's who are not the low bidders for their trades

In minority outreach programs the requirement is not to meet a quota, but to demonstrate sufficient efforts to obtain MBE'S and WBE's. Since efforts must be demonstrated by paperwork, bid protests are resolved by agency staff minutely examining MBE/WBE outreach paperwork submitted by each bidder. Reported cases show that agencies have determined the qualifications of bidders based on such factors as the number of telephone calls made in attempts to persuade MBE's and WBE's to submit bids, the amount of time taken up on the telephone in these persuasive efforts, and the persistence of the bidder in trying to make sure that faxes inviting participation are delivered.

Disappointed low bidders whose bids are rejected because of insufficient outreach efforts may allege bureaucratic nit-picking and point out that evaluation of outreach efforts offers the agency an opportunity to award work to a favored bidder and therefore the MBE and WBE outreach programs can be a screen for favoritism and corruption. Much attention is also devoted to screening contractors who claim to be minority or women owned and controlled. It is not easy to penetrate the paperwork defenses of a contractor who is determined to make it appear that a business is minority or women owned and controlled when, in actuality, it is owned and controlled by a white man or white men.

4. Minorities vs. Women: Do the Same Concepts Apply?

Much ink has been spilled on the question of whether the Supreme Court will treat women and minorities the same. Slavery is a big part of the constitutional justification for minority preferences, so obviously the same reasoning does not necessarily also apply to women and other minorities as applies to blacks. In many states the MBE/WBE question has become politicized. The legal and political environment is fluid and contractors are well advised to keep up-to-date with the latest developments in the agencies with which they wish to do business.

An interesting development is the emergence of "MBE-WBE compliance providers" who, for a fee, write the letters, place the ads, send the faxes, make the phone calls, keep the records, and create the paperwork to show good faith efforts. This development, which to some is a cynical exploitation of a serious social problem, seems to others to show a simple response to changing market factors.

5. Prevailing Wages

Contractors on most public projects are required to pay prevailing wages. The labor departments of states establish the prevailing wage for journeymen, apprentices, and helpers in the various trades. The prevailing wages are published as part of the contract documents on public projects and the prime contractor and subcontractors are required to pay them. If a subcontractor fails to pay prevailing wages, the agency penalizes the prime contractor and the prime contractor penalizes the subcontractor. In addition to being required to pay backpay to affected workers, the contractor also forfeits to the agency a daily penalty for each worker as to whom there was a failure to pay prevailing wages. (Penalties vary from state to state: $50 to $100 per day per worker is common.)

Contractors are required to keep records showing payment of prevailing wages, known as "certified payrolls", and to make copies of the certified payrolls available to the prime contractor, the agency, and any member of the public. This requirement enables union agents to police the payment of prevailing wages by non-union contractors.

The presence in many states of qualified workers who are willing to work for less than prevailing wages makes it difficult to enforce the laws on all projects. When a local agency does bring charges against a contractor, the contractor is considered guilty until proven innocent. Many prime contractors, in an attempt to protect themselves against defaulting subcontractors, require every worker on the jobsite to sign an affidavit every day to authenticate compliance with prevailing wage requirements. The reported cases include amusing incidents where workers have been required by their employers to conceal themselves in tool boxes and trash bins to avoid detection by inspecting authorities. A common ruse is for a contractor to issue checks that comply with prevailing wage requirements, and to require workers to endorse and return the checks to the employer, who then pays less than prevailing wages in cash.

The prime contractor is authorized to withhold from a subcontractor who violates prevailing wage requirements back wages and penalties incurred, and a subcontractor who wishes to challenge the amount withheld must comply with the requirements of a short statute of limitations: typically 90 days.

Case in Point

Contractors have done strange things in an attempt to avoid payment of prevailing wages. One contractor passed checks to workers upside-down so they could not see the amounts of the checks, and directed the workers to endorse the checks and then paid them in cash. Workers were instructed to hide in the toolshed when state inspectors came to the jobsite. One painter was paid $4.15 an hour rather than the prevailing hourly rate of $26 per hour, while Bok Chung Kim, a carpenter's helper, was required to sign timesheets that falsely stated he was paid $24 per hour and worked only three days when he had actually worked five days. In such a case, a California court held that the contractor was guilty of a felony. People v Hwang, 25 Cal App 4th 1168 (1994).

LEGAL TERMS

Abandonment. The failure of both parties to a contract to abide by its terms.

Acceptance. Manifestation that a party assents to a contract.

Accord and Satisfaction. Conduct of a debtor that indicates agreement to an amount of money owed by the debtor to a creditor.

Act of God. An unexpected event, not within the control of either party, that makes the performance of contract impossible, unreasonable, or illegal.

ADR. Alternative Dispute Resolution. Resolution of a dispute without litigation.

Affidavit. A written statement that is made under oath.

Agent. One who is authorized to act on behalf of a principal.

All Risk Policy. A property insurance policy that insures against all risks of loss that are not specifically excluded.

Ambiguous. An expression that has more than one meaning.

Anticipatory Breach. A positive statement by a party to a contract that the party will not perform the terms of the contract.

Arbitration. A proceeding for resolution of disputes in which a neutral person, after hearing evidence presented by both sides, makes a final and binding decision that resolves the dispute.

Assignment. Transfer of the rights and duties under a contract from one party to another.

Attorney. A person with legal learning who is authorized to act on behalf of a client.

Award. A written decision signed by an arbitrator that resolves a dispute that has been submitted to arbitration by the parties to the dispute.

Backcharge. An offsetting charge against a bill, often asserted by an owner against a prime contractor or a by prime contractor against a subcontractor based on assertedly defective construction work.

Bankruptcy. A legal proceeding by which a debtor may avoid legal obligations.

Bid. An offer to perform; an offer to enter into a contract.

Breach of Contract. A material failure to perform an act required by contract.

Caveat Emptor. "Let the buyer beware."

Change Order. An order to change the work to be performed under a construction contract, usually given an owner to a prime contractor or a by prime contractor to a subcontractor.

Chattel. Moveable personal property.

Cloud. A defect in the title to real property.

Collateral. Property in the possession of a creditor to guarantee payment by a debtor.

Common Enemy Doctrine. The legal doctrine that flood waters are a common enemy and that property owners may fight to protect their property regardless of the damage to neighboring property.

Comparative Negligence. The legal doctrine that wrongdoers should pay damages proportional to their fault.

Compensatory Damages. An amount calculated to compensate a party for economic loss caused by the wrongful act of another.

Condominium. Ownership of space in a structure along with a common interest, with other owners, in facilities that serve the structure.

Consideration. A benefit flowing from a promisee to a promisor in exchange for the promisor's agreement to perform an act.

Construction Lender. An institution or individual that lends money to a borrower for the purpose of constructing improvements to real property.

Contract of Adhesion. A term of a contract offered to a person of inferior bargaining position who has no effective means of negotiating more favorable terms.

Covenant. A promise.

Cross Examination. Questions framed to undermine the testimony of a witness.

Damages. 1) Injuries; 2) an amount of money awarded to a plaintiff to compensate for loss caused by the wrongful conduct of a defendant.

Deed of Trust. Mortgage.

Default. A material failure to perform the requirements of a contract.

Deposition. The extra-judicial testimony of a witness given under oath; the written record thereof.

Diminution in Value. The amount by which the market of property is reduced by a wrongful act.

Direct Examination. Questions directed to a friendly witness.

Discovery. A process in which parties to a lawsuit are made to divulge information.

Dismissal. The act of dropping a lawsuit.

Drawings. Plans.

Due Process. Notice, and an opportunity to be heard.

Duress. Compulsion.

Easement. A right to utilize real property owned by another.

Embezzlement. Theft of property in the legal possession of the thief.

Encroachment. Personal property of one person intruding upon real estate owned by another.

Encumbrance. A charge against real property.

Equitable Lien. A lien that is given to an improver of property to prevent the unjust enrichment of a property owner or a construction lender.

Equity. The prevention of injustice that might result from strict enforcement of law.

Escrow. A neutral facilitator who follows the instructions of parties to a transaction.

Estimate. (n) A prediction of the cost of performing work.

Estoppel. The doctrine that a person may not contradict his own positive representations.

Evidence. Testimony, documents, and things introduced in a proceeding to support the contentions of the parties.

Exculpatory Clause. A provision in a contract that relieves a party of liability.

Exemplary Damages. Damages awarded to a private litigant and against a defendant to punish the wrongdoing of the defendant.

Exhibit. A document or thing that is offered as evidence in a proceeding.

Ex Parte Proceeding. One party to a dispute appears before a judge when the other is not present.

Extra Work. Work performed by a contractor that is not included within the scope of the work defined by the contract documents.

FAA. Federal Arbitration Act.

Fiduciary. (n) A person in a relationship of trust.

Force Majeure. An overwhelming, but unanticipated event.

Fraud. A false statement of fact that is designed to deceive.

General Partner. A member of a partnership with unlimited management authority and liability.

Guarantee. An undertaking that a thing will or will not happen.

Hearing. A proceeding conducted by a judge or arbitrator who receives evidence about a dispute.

Hearsay. Evidence of an event that the witness did not personally perceive.

Illegal. Contrary to law.

Immune. Not subject to legal process.

Implied Contract. A contract that is not in words.

Implied Covenant. A promise that is not expressed in a contract, but that is implied from the surrounding circumstances.

Implied Indemnity. An obligation to indemnify that arises not from the words of a contract, but from the circumstances of the parties.

Implied Warranty. A promise, usually related to a the quality or serviceability of goods, that is not in words but is implied from the circumstances of a sale.

Impossibility. A doctrine of contract law that excuses performance that becomes physically impossible.

Indemnity. A promise to hold a person harmless from liability or loss.

Independent Contractor. A person who, in performing services for another, is responsible only for the final result, and is not subject to control as to the methods used to achieve that result.

Injunction. A court order that requires a party to do or not to do a certain act.

Insolvency. Liabilities exceed assets.

Interrogatories. Written questions that a party to litigation must answer in writing, under oath.

Joint Check. A check made payable to more than one payee.

Joint Control. An independent escrow used to safeguard and disburse construction funds.

Joint Venture. A partnership whose business is limited to the pursuit of a particular project.

Judgment. A final decision of a court.

Latent Ambiguity. A term of a contract that appears on its face to be unambiguous, but that is rendered ambiguous by external circumstances.

Latent Defect. A construction defect that is not perceptible by ordinary observation.

Lateral Support. A force that prevents land from moving in a lateral direction.

Law. A rule of conduct enforced by courts.

Lawsuit. A proceeding in which the jurisdiction of a court is invoked to resolve to a dispute between two or more parties.

Lawyer. A person who is learned in, and authorized to practice, law.

Liability. Legal responsibility.

Liability Insurance. Insurance that will pay damages for which the insured becomes liable.

Limited Partnership. A partnership in which the management authority and liability of some of the partners is limited.

Liquidated Damages. An amount determined by contract in advance of injury to be paid to compensate a party for an injury.

Lis Pendens. A document recorded in the county recorder's office that gives public notice of litigation involving title to or the possession of real property.

Lump Sum Contract. A contract in which the amount to be paid to the contractor is agreed in advance to be a stipulated sum.

Malice. Desire to do harm; anger, hatred.

Malicious Prosecution. Pursuing a lawsuit without probable cause.

Malpractice. Negligent act or omission of a professional.

Materialman. Supplies construction materials to a project.

Mechanics Lien. A charge against real estate for the value of work or materials incorporated thereon.

Misconduct. Wrongful conduct.

Mistake. A legal doctrine under which formation of a contract may be prevented if a party entered into the contract under a material mistake of fact.

Modification. An agreed change to the terms of a contract.

Mortgage. A lien against real estate that secures payment of a debt.

Motion. Application to a judge or arbitrator for an order.

Municipal Affairs. Government activities that are subject to the control of a municipality.

Mutual Assent. An objective manifestation by parties that they intend to be bound by a contract.

Mutuality. The concept that a contract, to be enforceable at all, must be enforceable by both parties.

Negligence. The failure to exercise due care.

Neutral. A neutral arbitrator.

Neutral Arbitrator. An arbitrator not controlled by or biased in favor of any party.

Notice. Delivery of information to a party.

Nuisance. A condition of or on real property that damages neighboring persons or property.

Offer. A promise that is enforceable if accepted.

Offeror. A person who makes an offer.

Offsite Improvement. Improvements, located away from the site of a structure, that serve that structure.

Oral Agreement. A contract in words that are not reduced to writing.

Ordinance. A law enacted by a city or a county.

Original Contractor. In the law of mechanics liens, a contractor who contracts directly with an owner of real property.

Owner-Builder. An owner of property who undertakes to construct improvements thereon but does not employ a general contractor.

Parol Evidence Rule. "The meaning of a contract cannot be changed by reference to statements made by the parties to the contract before the contract was formed."

Partisan Arbitrator. An arbitrator controlled by, appointed by, or biased in favor of a party to a dispute.

Partnership. A business organization in which the owners are mutually responsible for management and liability.

Patent Ambiguity. An expression in a document that is obviously susceptible to more than one interpretation.

Patent Defect. A vice or shortcoming in a structure that is apparent to reasonable inspection.

Payment. Satisfaction, or partial satisfaction, of a debt.

Payment Bond. An undertaking by a surety that those persons who supply work and materials to a construction project will be paid for the work and materials.

Payment Schedule. A document, usu. attached to a construction contract, that specifies the times for, and amounts of, payments for construction services.

Payroll. The record of wages, salaries, and fringe benefits paid by an employer to its employees.

Peculiar Risk Doctrine. The doctrine that an owner, by employing an independent contractor, cannot escape liability to persons who may be injured during construction operations on the owner's property, since the construction operations involve a special risk of harm.

Penalty Clause. A clause in a construction contract by which a contractor is assessed with a monetary penalty, usually on a daily basis, for delay in the completion of a project.

Performance Bond. An undertaking by a surety that a contractor will perform a contract.

Perjury. Lying under oath.

Personal Property. Property that is not attached to real estate.

Plans. Drawings in which it is assumed that the observer is situated above the thing represented.

Pleadings. Formal written documents, filed with a court, accusing a party of wrongdoing, or defending a party against such an accusation.

Prevailing Wage Law. A law that establishes minimum wages for job classifications in the construction trades.

Prime Contractor. A general contractor who contracts with a property owner and, in turn, employs a subcontractor or subcontractors to perform some or all of the work.

Privity. Persons who have contractual relationships with each other are in privity.

Procedure. Rules governing court operations.

Progressive Loss. An injury to person or property that occurs over a period of time, such as cracking caused by gradual settlement of soils or illness caused by inhalation of dust.

Promise. An undertaking that something will or will not happen in the future.

Promisee. A person to whom a promise is made.

Promisor. A person who makes a promise.

Promissory Estoppel. A promise that is enforceable even though it is not supported by consideration, since the promisor is estopped to withdraw it.

Promissory Note. A written promise to pay a sum on or before a particular date.

Proof of Service. Evidence that a legal document has been delivered to a specified person.

Property. A tangible thing that is, or may be, possessed by a person.

Property Damage. Injury to tangible property.

Property Insurance. Insurance against damage to, or loss of, property that belongs to the insured.

Pro Rata. Proportionate.

Provisional Remedies. Orders or proceedings that protect persons or property while legal proceedings are pending.

Publication. The process of making writings or drawings available for distribution to or inspection by the public.

Punitive Damages. Damages awarded to a private person against a wrongdoer by way of punishment, and to deter future misconduct.

Quasi Contract. application of contract rules of law to parties that do not have a contractual relationship.

Real Estate. Land that is subject to ownership, with its permanent improvements and appurtenances.

Real Property. Land that is subject to ownership, with its permanent improvements and appurtenances.

Reasonable Use. A legal doctrine that allocates water rights.

Receiver. An officer of the court who administers property pending resolution of dispute between claimants to the property.

Recreational Use Statutes. Laws that have been adopted in most states to protect property owners from liability to persons who are permitted to use the property for recreational purposes.

Regulations. Laws that are enacted by a public administrative agency, rather than by an elected legislative body.

Relief. Damages or court orders awarded in litigation.

Rental Value. A measure of damages for deprivation of the use of property.

Rescission. A legal remedy for a material breach of contract under which the law pretends that a contract never existed and attempts to put the parties in the positions they occupied before the contract was executed: CANCELLATION.

Res Judicata. The doctrine that courts will not re-litigate the same issues between the same parties.

Respondiat Superior. The doctrine that a principal is liable for the acts of an agent, and an employer for the acts of an employee.

Security Interest. An interest in property, real or personal, held by a creditor to secure the performance of an obligation.

Setoff. An offset against a claim.

Severability. A rule under which a contract may be divided into its component parts.

Slander of Title. Intentionally and wrongfully placing a cloud on title to real estate.

Sovereign Immunity. The doctrine that the sovereign is immune to litigation, originally applied to monarchs and now applied to governments.

Specialty Contractor. A contractor who follows a recognized trade: TRADE CONTRACTOR.

Specifications. A description of systems, materials, and facilities to be employed in building a structure, and incorporated into a contract for construction.

Statute of Frauds. A statute that requires certain contracts to be evidenced by a writing.

Statute of Limitations. The period of time after a cause of action arises before the expiration of which a plaintiff must file suit, or lose the right to do so.

Statute of Repose. A statute of limitations, us. measured from the completion of a work of improvement, protecting builders, contractors, architects, and engineers from liability for defects in the construction of the improvement.

Stop Notice. A charge against construction funds in the hands of a property owner or a construction lender for the value of work or materials incorporated into a construction project.

Strict Liability. Liability without fault, us. imposed by the courts for social reasons to distribute the risk of injury to consumers by imposing on the manufacturers of products liability for injury caused by the use of those products even though the manufacturer is not shown to be at fault.

Subdivider. One who buys land wholesale and sells it retail.

Submission Agreement. An agreement between parties to a dispute by means of which the dispute is submitted to arbitration.

Substantial Compliance. A doctrine that may excuse minor violations of licensing statutes.

Substantial Performance. The doctrine that a contract is enforceable by a party who has not strictly complied with all requirements of a contract, but who has substantially complied therewith.

Sue and Labor Clause. A clause in a property insurance policy that authorizes the insured to expend funds to protect the insured property.

Summary Judgment. A judgment awarded on the basis of affidavits and legal briefing rather than on the basis of evidence introduced at a trial.

Supplier. One who supplies construction materials to a project.

Surety. One who undertakes to guarantee performance by another.

Surface Waters. Rain water collected and running on the surface of the land rather than being confined to drains and water courses.

Temporary Restraining Order. An order of brief duration issued by a court pending a hearing on the merits.

Testimony. Oral evidence offered by a witness in the course of a hearing, a trial, or a deposition.

Third Party Beneficiary. A person who is not a party to a contract but who is the intended beneficiary thereof and may therefore enforce it.

Title Insurance. A guarantee of title issued by an insurance company.

Tort. A negligent or intentional wrongful act that damages the person or property of another the wrongful nature of which is independent of any contractual relationship.

Total Cost. A method of computing damages sustained by a contractor because of breaches of contract causing the contractor to operate in an inefficient or unproductive manner.

Transition Lot. A lot in a subdivision that consists of both cut and fill.

Trespass. Unauthorized entry upon the real property of another.

Trial. A hearing conducted by a judge at which litigants are entitled to introduce evidence and arguments supporting, and defending against, claims.

Trust Deed. A document evidencing a security interest in real property: MORTGAGE.

Uncertainty. The doctrine that contracts are unenforceable if unintelligible

Unconscionability. A doctrine that courts will not enforce contractual provisions that put one party at the mercy of another.

Uniform Commercial Code. A statute governing commercial transactions, sales, and commercial paper that has been adopted in substantially the same form in all 50 states.

Unjust Enrichment. A situation in which one party is unjustly enriched at the expense of another party.

Usury. Collecting, or contracting to collect, interest at higher than the lawful rate.

Waiver. The intentional relinquishment of a known right.

Witness. A person who observed events and is called to testify concerning those events at a hearing.

Work Product Exclusion. A provision in a liability insurance policy that withholds coverage for damages to work performed by or on behalf of the insured.

Workers Compensation. A system established by statute under which employers are responsible for medical expenses and disabilities of workers injured while on the job. Compensation is payable even if the employer is not at fault and even if the carelessness of the worker contributed to the injury, but the employer is not liable for damages for pain and suffering.

Wrongful Death. Unlawful homicide, whether negligent or intentional.

CONSTRUCTION TERMS

ABS Pipe. A plastic pipe sold in 10 and 20 foot lengths in different diameters for stacks and main drains and is used only for drain lines.

Acoustical Block. A masonry block used for its sound-absorbing qualities.

Acoustical Tile. Ceiling panels in board form used for its sound absorbing properties. Sometimes used on walls.

Acoustical Treatment. The act or process of applying acoustical materials to walls and ceilings.

Acrylic. A general class of resinous polymers derived from esters, amides or other acrylic aid derivatives. A transparent plastic material used in sheet form for glazing windows and skylights.

Addenda. A revision in the contract document made prior to the execution of the owner-contractor contract.

Adhesion. The state in which two surfaces are held together by interfacial forces which may consist of valence forces or interlocking action, or both.

Admixture. A material other than water, aggregates, and hydraulic cement used as an ingredient of concrete or mortar, and added immediately before or during its mixing. A chemical additive used to alter the normal properties of concrete.

Aggregate. Inert particles such as sand, gravel, crushed stone, or expanded materials, in a concrete or plaster mixture. Granular material, such as sand, gravel, crushed stone, and iron blast-furnace slag, used with a cementing medium to form a hydraulic-cement, concrete or mortar.

Air Change Method. A method of calculating the quantity of infiltration air into a building. This method is used when construction quality cannot be determined and are based on medium quality of construction.

Air Eliminator. A mechanical device that expels excess air.

Air Entraining Agent. A substance added to concrete, mortar or cement that produces air bubbles during mixing, making it easier to work with, and increasing its resistance to frost.

Air Plenum. Any space used to convey air in a building or structure. The space above a suspended ceiling is often used as an air plenum.

Air-Handling System. A system to heat, cool, humidity, dehumidify, filter and transport air. It consists of an air handling unit, fresh air (F.A.) and exhaust air (E.A.) damper at the building exterior, ductwork, supply air (S.A.), diffusers or registers, and return air (R.A.) grills in the conditioned space.

Alkali. A chemical substance which effectively neutralizes acid material so as to form neutral salts. A

base. The opposite of acid. Examples are ammonia and caustic soda.

Alternates. A stipulated construction sum, in addition to the base bid, for specific items to be included or excluded from the project.

Ambient Sound. The quiet-state noise level in a room or space, which is a composite of sounds from many external sources, both near and far, over which one individual has no control.

Anchor Bolt. A bolt embedded in concrete for the purpose of fastening a building frame to a concrete or masonry foundation.

Anchorage. An attachment for resistance to movement. The movement can be a result of overturning, sliding or uplift. The most common anchorage for these movements are tie-downs (hold-downs) for overturning and uplift, and anchor bolts for sliding.

Annunciator Panel. A panel mounted on a surface which indicates by lights which circuits have been activated.

Anodized. A metal that has been subjected to electrolytic action in order to coat with a protective or decorative film.

Anti-siphon. A device to prevent the removal of fluid caused by suction produced by fluid flow.

Application for Payment. A written document forwarded by the contractor requesting payment for work completed.

Arch. A curved structure in which compression is the essential cause of internal stresses. A structural member with an upward-curved centerline axis and a relatively small cross section, supported so that the distance between its ends cannot change.

Aseismic Region. A region that is relatively free of earthquakes.

Ashlar. Masonry composed of squared stones; one pattern of masonry construction.

Asphalt. A residue in petroleum or coal-tar refining that is used for pavements and as a waterproofing cement.

Asphalt-Saturated Felt. A moisture-resistant sheet material, available in several different thicknesses, usually consisting of a heavy paper that has been impregnated with asphalt.

ASTM. American Society for Testing and Materials, 1916 Race Street, Philadelphia, PA 19103, (215) 299-5420.

Attenuation Blanket. Material utilized to help in the reduction of the energy or intensity of sound.

Axial. In a direction parallel to the long axis of a structural member. In line with the axis. An axial force causes tension or compression stress over the cross section of a member.

Backfill. Earth or earthen material used to fill the excavation around a foundation; the act of filling around a foundation.

Backflow Preventer. A device which prevents sewage from the building's sewer from flowing backward into the plumbing fixture(s).

Ballast. A device used with a fluorescent and high intensity lamp, to provide the necessary circuit condition for starting and operation.

Baluster. Vertical members that extend from a stair, or floor, to a handrail. A small pillar or column used to support a rail.

Batch Plant. An operating installation of equipment including batchers and mixers as required for batching or for batching and mixing concrete materials; also called mixing plant when equipment is included.

Batter Board. A temporary framework used to assist in locating the corners when laying a foundation. Also used to maintain proper elevations of excavations and trenches in any kind of below ground construction.

Batter Pile. Pile driven at an angle to brace a structure against lateral thrust.

Bay. A rectangular area of a building defined by four adjacent columns; a portion of a building that projects from a facade.

Beam. A straight structural member that acts primarily to resist transverse loads. A structural element which sustains transverse loading and develops internal forces of bending and shear in resisting the loads. An inclusive term for joists, girders, rafters, and purlins.

Beam Chair. A wire seat or support for reinforcing bars designed to maintain their location while concrete for a beam is poured around them.

Beam Hanger. A strap wire or other device used to hang beam forms from another structural member.

Bearing Pad. A block of plastic or synthetic rubber used to cushion the point at which one element rests upon another.

Bearing Wall. A wall which supports any vertical loads in addition to its own weight.

Bellows. An instrument or machine that draws in air through a valve or orifice by expansion and contraction and expels it through a tube.

Bending. The result of a force which tends to cause curvature in a linear element. Internal stresses of tension and compression are a result of this action.

Bending Moment. The sum of moments for all forces that occur above the neutral axis. The moment that causes a beam or other structural member to bend.

Bending Stress. A compressive or tensile stress resulting from the application of a nonaxial force to a structural member.

Bid Bond. A bond, secured by the bidder, which guarantees that the bidder selected by the owner will accept the project, or the owner will have the project for the bid price as noted in the accepted bid.

Bitumen. A tar based mixture, such as asphalt or coal tar.

Bituminous. Resembling, containing, or impregnated with various mixtures of hydrocarbons (like tar) together with their nonmetallic derivatives.

Bloom. A visible exudation or efflorescence on the surface.

Board Foot. A unit of lumber volume, a rectangular solid nominally 12" x 12" x 1". The equivalent of a board 1 foot square and 1 inch thick.

BOCA. Building Officials and Code Administrators International, an organization that publishes a model building code.

Bollard. Short steel post (usually filled with concrete) set to prevent vehicular access or to protect property from damage by vehicular encroachment. Steel or cast iron post to which ships are tied.

Bond. The adherence of one material to another. Effective bonds must be achieved between the mortar and scratch coat, between the tile and mortar, and between the adhesive and backing.

Bond Beam. A horizontal grouted element within masonry in which reinforcement is embedded.

Bond Breaker. A material used to prevent adhesion of newly placed concrete and the substrate.

Bonding Agent. A substance applied to a suitable substrate to create a bond between it and a succeeding layer as between a subsurface and a terrazzo topping or a succeeding plaster application.

Borrow. Excavated material that has been taken from one area to be used as fill at another location.

Box Beam. A bending member of metal or plywood which, in cross section, resembles a closed rectangular box.

Box Culvert. A concrete drainage structure rectangular-shaped, reinforced and cast either in place or precast in sections.

Broom Finish. A finish applied to an uncured concrete surface, to provide skid or slip resistance, made by dragging a broom across the freshly placed concrete surface.

Brown Coat. The second of three coats of a plaster or stucco application.

Building Envelope. Elements of the building, including all external building materials, windows, and walls, that enclose the internal space.

Building Official. The official charged with administration and enforcement of the applicable building code, or his duly authorized representative.

Building Paper. Water repellent paper used to assist in shedding incidental moisture what may penetrate exterior finishes of exterior wall construction. Thick paper, used to insulate a building before the siding or cladding is installed. Occasionally used in flooring between double floors.

Built-Up Roof. A roof covering made of continuous rolls or sheets of saturated or coated felt. They are then cemented together with asphalt and may have a final coating of gravel or slag.

Bull Float. A tool comprising a large, flat, rectangular piece of wood, aluminum, or magnesium usually 8 in. (20 cm) wide and 42 to 60 in. (100 to 150 cm) long, and a handle 4 to 16 ft. (1 to 5 m) in length used to smooth unformed surfaces of freshly placed concrete.

Bullnose. A trim tile with a convex radius on one edge. This tile is used for finishing the top of a wainscot or for turning an outside corner.

Bullnose Corner. A type of bullnose trim with a convex radius on two adjacent edges.

Bullnose Glazed. A trim tile with a convex radius on one edge that has been given a glassy or glossy surface.

Bumper, Dock. Thick rubber units placed under loading dock openings to absorb the shock and prevent damage when trucks back in for loading or unloading.

Buoyant Uplift. The force of water or liquefied soil that tends to raise a building foundation out of the ground.

Bus Bar. A large, flat conductor, usually solid copper, used for carrying very high electrical currents. An uninsulated bar or tube used as an electrical conductor at a circuit junction.

Bus Duct. A prefabricated unit containing one or more electric conductors, often a metal bar, that serves as a common connection for two or more circuits.

Bus Ground. In the main electrical service panel, where the neutral service wire (generally white) attaches and is linked to the earth by the ground wire.

Bush Hammer. A hammer that has a rectangular head with serrated or jagged faces. The bush hammer is used for roughing concrete.

Bushing. A removable cylindrical lining for an opening used to limit the size of an opening, resist abrasion, or serve as a guide. An electrically insulating lining for a hole to protect a through conductor.

Butt Hinge. A hinge consisting of two plates with a removable connecting pin.

Butt Joint. A plain square joint between two members.

Buttering Trowel. The blade of the buttering trowel is approximately 4-1/2" wide and 7" long. It is used in buttering rich mortar to masonry, a method commonly used in the eastern states.

Butyl Caulking. Synthetic rubber caulking dispensed in a tube made by polymerizing isobutylene.

BX Cable. Type of indoor wiring consisting of two or more insulated wires protected by a wound, galvanized steel strip cover. The metal winding forms a flexible tube.

Cable Bus. An assembly of insulated cables.

Cable Tray. Open track support forces heavily insulated cables.

Caisson. A cylindrical, sitecast concrete foundation that penetrates through unsatisfactory soil to rest upon an underlying stratum of rock or satisfactory soil.

Camber. A deflection that is intentionally built into a structural element or form to improve appearance or to nullify the deflection of the element under the effects of loads, shrinkage and creep. A radius built into a given member to compensate for deflection. A light initial curvature in a beam or slab.

Cant Strip. A strip of material, usually treated wood or fiber, with a sloping face used to ease the transition from a horizontal to a vertical surface at the edge of a flat roof.

Cantilever. A beam, truss, or slab that extends beyond its last point of support. A beam which is supported only at one end.

Cantilever Wall. A retaining wall in which the wall and footing resists earth pressure by cantilever effect.

Cantilevered Beam. A beam that is supported at one end only.

Cap, Pile. A structural member usually fastened to, and placed on the top of a slender timber, concrete or structural element. Used to transmit loads into the pile or group of piles and to connect them.

Capacitor. A device which introduces capacitance into an electric circuit.

Casement. A window in which the sash opens upon hinges.

Casement Window. A window that pivots on an axis, along the vertical line of the frame.

Casework. Assembled cabinetry or millwork.

Casing. The wood finish pieces surrounding the frame of a window or door, or the finished lumber around a post or beam. A cylindrical steel tube used to line a drilled or driven hole in foundation work.

Cast Iron Pipe. Pipe that is manufactured with an alloy of iron, carbon and silicon that is cast in a mold and is more easily fusible than steel.

Cast-In-Place. Mortar or concrete which is deposited in the place where it is required to harden as part of the structure, as opposed to precast concrete.

Castellated Beam. A steel, wide-flange section whose web has been cut along a zigzag path and reassembled by welding in such a way as to create a deeper section.

Casting Bed. A form in which precast concrete units are constructed.

Catch Basin. Formed pan, usually constructed of sheet metal to collect moisture and dirt which comes through grating. Basin usually includes drain connected to plumbing system.

Ceiling And Wall. A type of building framing construction.

Ceiling Joist. The vertical members in a building or structure upon which the roof rafters are attached.

Cell. A void space having a gross cross-sectional area greater than 1-1/2 square inches (967 mm2).

Cement Plaster. Plaster used on exterior surfaces or in damp areas. Plaster having Portland Cement as a binder.

Cement, Portland. A hydraulic cement produced by pulverizing clinker consisting essentially of hydraulic calcium silicates, and usually containing one or more of the forms of calcium sulfate as an interground addition.

Cementitious. Having cementing properties; usually used with reference to inorganic substances, such as portland cement and lime.

Center Pole, Steel. Column in enter of spiral stair which supports stair treads.

Centigrade. A scale of temperature which features 0 degree and 100 degree as the freezing and boiling point of water respectively. To convert centigrade to Fahrenheit multiply by 1.8 and add 32 e.g. (100 degree x 1.8)--32=212 degree F.

Certificate For Payment. A written document forwarded to the general contractor by the architect, engineer, or owner approving payment for work completed.

Certificate for Substantial Completion. A written document forwarded to the general contractor by the architect, engineer, or owner indicating that the project is substantially complete. This document initiates the time period for the final payment to the contractor.

Certificate of Insurance. A certificate provided by the general contractor verifying that he has obtained the required insurance for the project.

CFM. Cubic feet per minute.

Chair. A device used to support reinforcing bars.

Chamfer. A beveled surface cut on the edge of a piece of wood. A strip of wood or other substance cut on an angle and placed in concrete formwork to create a beveled finished surface on the corners of the final concrete shape (beam, column, etc.).

Chamfer Strip. An insert that is triangular or curved, placed in an inside corner to produce a rounded or flat beveled edge at the right angle corner of a construction member.

Channel. A steel or aluminum section shaped like a rectangular box with one side removed.

Check Valve. A device which allows fluid or air to pass through in only one direction. A valve which prevents the back-flow of water or other liquid by automatically closing.

Checking. Short shallow cracks on the surface.

Chicken Wire. Thin, woven wire mounted on an exterior wall as a base for stucco plaster to cling to.

Chiller. A piece of equipment that contains a compressor, condenser and evaporator tank. It produces chilled water for circulation through a building.

Chord. One of the main members of a truss, usually horizontal, and braced by web members of the truss. Perimeter member of a building or structure which resists lateral forces.

Circuit Breaker. An overcurrent protection device.

Class A, B, C, Roofing. Roof covering materials classified according to their resistance to fire when tested in accordance with ASTM E108. Class A is the highest, and Class C is the lowest.

Clay Pipe. Pipe used for drainage systems and sanitary sewers made of earthenware and glazed to eliminate porosity.

Clay Tile Floor. (Earthenware) Quarry tile that is fired and used for flooring.

Cleanout. An opening to the bottom of a grout space of sufficient size and spacing to allow the removal of debris.

Clevis Hanger. A U-shaped metal hanger with the ends drilled to receive a pin or bolt used for attaching or suspending parts.

Closer. The last masonry unit laid in a course; a partial masonry unit used at the corner of a course to adjust the joint spacing.

Closure Strip. A resilient strip, used to close openings created by joining metal panels and flashing.

CMU. Concrete Masonry Unit

Coated Roof. A roof usually flat, that has an asphaltic material applied to it to seal against the elements.

Cofferdam. A watertight enclosure from which water is pumped to expose the bottom of a body of water and permit construction.

Cold Joint. Any point in a tile installation when tile and setting bed have terminated and the surface has lost its plasticity before work is continued. The joint formed between hardened concrete and freshly poured concrete.

Collar. A compression ring around a small circular opening.

Collar Joint. The vertical mortar joint between wythes of masonry.

Collar Tie. A piece of wood nailed across two opposing rafters near the ridge to resist wind uplift.

Collector. A force transfer element that collects loads from a diaphragm (horizontal element) and transfers them to the shear walls (vertical element).

Column. A member used primarily to support axial compression loads and with a height of at least three times its least lateral dimension. An upright structural member acting primarily in compression. A member which is subjected primarily to axial forces. A square, rectangular, or cylindrical support for roofs, ceilings, and so forth, composed of base, shaft, and capital.

Column Pier. A foundation member of plain or reinforced concrete to support a column.

Column Tie. A single loop of steel bar, usually bent into a rectangular configuration, used to tie a concrete column.

Compaction. The process whereby the volume of freshly placed mortar or concrete is reduced to the minimum practical space usually by vibration, centrifugation, tamping, or some combination of these; to mold it within forms or molds and around embedded parts and reinforcement, and to eliminate voids other than entrained air.

Composite Beam. A beam that is composed of two different materials; for example, a wood and a steel beam, or a steel beam and concrete slab, in which the two act as one.

Composite Concrete Flexure Members. The concrete flexural members of pre-cast and cast-in-place concrete elements constructed in separate units but so interconnected that all units respond to a load(s) as a unit.

Compression. Force which tends to crush adjacent particles of a material together and cause overall shortening in the direction of its action. Stress which tends to shorten a member.

Concrete. A composite material which consists essentially of a binding medium within which are embedded particles or fragments of aggregate; in portland cement concrete, the binder is a mixture of portland cement and water. A mixture of cement, water, fine aggregate (and), and coarse aggregate (gravel).

Concrete Admixture. A substance added to concrete to aid in imparting color, control workability, help in waterproofing, control setting and to entrain air.

Concrete Filled Pile. A long slender construction element filled with concrete, driven in the ground for the purpose of supporting a load.

Concrete Masonry Unit (CMU). A block of hardened concrete, with or without hollow cores, designed to be laid in the same manner as a brick; a concrete block.

Concrete, Precast. Cast and cured concrete in other than its final form. Examples are, precast concrete slabs, precast reinforced lintels, beams, columns, piles, parts of walls and floors, etc.

Concrete, Prestressed. Concrete in which internal stresses of such magnitude and distribution are introduced so that the tensile stresses resulting from the service loads are counteracted to a desired degree.

Concrete Topping. To provide durability, safety and beauty, a commercial mixture used to top concrete floor surfaces.

Concrete Waterproofing. An act or process of adding a material to concrete to make it impervious to water or dampness.

Concrete, Lightweight. Concrete that has substantially lower weight than that made from gravel or crushed stone.

Concrete, Structural Lightweight. Concrete containing lightweight aggregate, not exceeding 115 P.C.F.

Condensation. Usually refers to liquid drops which form when a vapor is chilled below its boiling point. Also refers to water droplets that deposit on surfaces whose temperature is below the dewpoint. The process of changing from a gaseous to a liquid state, especially as applied to water.

Condenser. A heat exchanger in a refrigeration cycle used to discharge heat to the outside. Three commonly used types of condensers can be classified as water cooled, air cooled, and evaporative. Condenser water is normally circulated through a cooling tower through which heat is distributed to the atmosphere. A heat exchanger in a refrigeration cycle used to discharge heat to the outside.

Conduit. A protective sleeve usually used for individual electrical cables.

Conduit, Flexible. Metallic conduit that is flexible and is put up in coils instead of lengths. May be used in lieu of the rigid type in most dry locations.

Conduit, Galvanized. Rigid or non-flexible conduit plated with zinc by a galvanized process.

Construction Change Directive. A document that directs a change in the work of the project, prepared by the architect and signed by the owner and architect. This change can adjust the contract sum and/or contract time. This document shall be used in the absence of total agreement on the terms of a change order.

Continuous Footing. A concrete footing that supports a wall or two or more columns. The footing can vary in width and depth.

Contraction Joint. Formed, sawed, or tooled groove in a concrete structure to create a weakened plane and regulate the location or cracking resulting from the dimensional change of different parts of the structure.

Control Joint. An intentional linear discontinuity in a structure or component, designed to form a plane of weakness where cracking can occur in response to various forces so as to minimize or eliminate cracking elsewhere in the structure.

Convection. Heat transferred by fluid motion.

Convector. A heat exchange device that uses the heat in steam, hot water, or an electric resistance element to warm the air in a room; often called, inaccurately, a radiator.

Corbel. A projection from the face of a beam, girder, column, or wall used as a beam seat or a decoration. A spanning device in which masonry units in successive courses are cantilevered slightly over one another; a project bracket of masonry or concrete. A masonry unit such as brick or stone which projects beyond the unit below.

Core Drilling. The process of drilling which extracts a cylindrical sample of concrete, rock or soil.

Corner Bead. A metal or plastic strip used to form a neat, durable edge at an outside corner of two walls of plaster or gypsum board.

Cornice. The exterior detail at the meeting of a wall and a roof overhang; a decorative molding at the intersection of a wall and a ceiling.

Corrosion. The eating and wearing away by chemical action (pitting, rusting).

Corrugated Panel. Metal or fiberglass sheeting formed into alternating ridges and valleys in parallel and applied as siding on a building or structure.

Counterflashing. An inverted L-shaped metal strip built into a wall to overlap flashing and make a roof watertight. A flashing turned down from above to overlap another flashing turned up from below so as to shed water. Strips of metal used to prevent water from entering the top edge of the vertical side of a roof flashing; they also allow expansion and contraction without danger of breaking the flashing.

Course. A horizontal layer of masonry units, one unit high; a horizontal line of shingles.

Cove. A trim tile unit having one edge with a concave radius. A cove is used to form a junction between the bottom wall course and the floor or to form an inside corner.

Coverage. A measure of the amount of material required to cover a given surface.

CPVC. Chlorinated Polyvinyl Chloride

Crack Length Method. A method of calculating the quantity of infiltration air into a building. This method requires specific information about dimensions and construction details of windows, doors, and other openings.

Crawling. A parting and contraction of the glaze on the surface of ceramic ware during drying or firing, resulting in unglazed areas bordered by coalesced glaze.

Crazing. The cracking which occurs in fired glazes or other ceramic coatings due to critical tensile stress.

Creep. Time-dependent deformation due to sustained load.

Creep. A permanent, inelastic, deformation in a material due to changes in the material caused by the prolonged application of structural stress. Plastic deformation that proceeds with time when certain materials, such as concrete, are subjected to constant, long-duration stress.

Creep (Seismic). Very slow periodic or episodic movement along a fault trace unaccompanied by earthquakes.

Cripple Stud. A wood wall-framing member that is shorter than full-length studs because it is interrupted by a header or sill.

Crown Molding. A type of molding used to make ceiling to wall transitions.

CRSI. Concrete Reinforcing Steel Institute, 933 N. Plum Grove Road, Schaumburg, IL 60173-4758, (708) 517-1200.

Culvert. A drain pipe or masonry crossing made of galvanized corrugated metal, aluminum, steel, or concrete constructed under a road or embankment to provide a waterway.

Curing. Maintenance of humidity and temperature of freshly placed concrete during some definite period following placing, casting, or finishing to assure satisfactory hydration of the cementitious materials and proper hardening of the concrete. The hardening of concrete or plaster.

Curing Blanket. A built-up covering of sacks, matting, hessian, straw, waterproof paper, or other suitable material placed over freshly finished concrete.

Curing Compound. A liquid that can be applied as a coating to the surface of newly placed concrete to retard the loss of water or, in the case of pigmented compounds, also to reflect heat so as to provide an opportunity for the concrete to develop its properties in a favorable temperature and moisture environment.

Curling. The distortion of an originally essentially linear or planar member into a curved shape such as the warping of a slab due to creep or to differences in temperature or moisture content in the zones adjacent to its opposite faces.

Curtain Wall. An exterior building wall that is supported, entirely by the frame of the building, rather than being self-supporting or loadbearing.

Cut and Fill. Excavated material removed from one location and used as fill material in another location.

Cylinder Test. A test to determine the compressive strength of concrete.

D-Cracking. The progressive formation on a concrete surface of a series of fine cracks at rather close intervals, often of random patterns, but in slabs on grade paralleling edges, joints, and cracks and usually curving across slab corners. (Also termed D-cracks and D-line cracks.)

D-Load. A constant load that in structures is due to the mass of the members, the supported structure, and permanent attachments or accessories.

Damper. A flap to control or obstruct the flow of gasses; specifically, a metal control flap in the throat of a fireplace, or in an air duct.

Damping. Dissipation of structure-borne noise by conversion to some other form of energy, usually heat. This usually is accomplished by using a material with a high internal energy-absorbing capacity.

Dampproofing. The treatment of concrete or mortar to help prevent the passage or absorption of water. Applied with a suitable coating to exposed surfaces or applied with a suitable admixture of treated cement.

Darby. A hand-manipulated straightedge, usually 3 to 8 ft. (1 to 2.5 m) long, used in the early stage leveling operations of concrete or plaster, preceding supplemental floating and finishing.

Daylighting. Illuminating the interior of a building by natural means.

DB. Decibel

Deadman. A large and/or heavy object buried in the ground as an anchor.

Deck. The form on which concrete for a slab is placed, also the floor or roof slab itself.

Deed Restrictions. Restrictive covenants often are included a deed which may limit future use(s) of the land, and other restrictions such as height, size, aesthetics, etc., as long as they are not against the public interest.

Deeds. A general term which refers to all documents conveying property, from one person to another.

Deflection. A variation in position or shape of a structure or structural element due to effects of loads or volume change, usually measured as a linear deviation from an established plane rather than an angular variation.

Deformation. A change in the shape of a structure or structural element caused by a load, or force, acting on the structure.

Degree Day Method. A method of computing fuel requirements for HVAC systems.

Degree of Saturation. The amount of water present in the air relative to the maximum amount it can hold at a given temperature without causing condensation.

Delamination. Separation of one layer from another.

Determinate. Having defined limits; definite. In structures, the condition of having exact sufficiency of stability, both externally and internally, therefore being determinable by the resolution of force alone. Short for statically determinate, meaning a structural system in which all the forces can be determined by the equations of statics alone.

Dewatering. To remove water from excavations with pumps, wellpoints or drainage systems.

Diaphragm. A thin, usually rectangular or square element of a structure that is capable of resisting lateral forces in its plane, such as a floor or roof.

Diaphragm Action. A bracing action that derives from the stiffness o a thin plane of material when it is loaded in a direction parallel to the plane. Diaphragms in buildings are typically floor, or roof surfaces of plywood, reinforced masonry, steel decking, or reinforced concrete.

Diffuser. A device for reducing the velocity and increasing the static pressure of a fluid passing through a system.

Direct Burial Conduit. Electric conduit suitable for burial in exterior applications with an outer surface that resists moisture, fungus, and corrosion.

Direct Current (DC). An electrical current that has a constant flow rate induced by a constant voltage.

Direct Drive Fan. A fan that is positively connected in line to a motor to operate at the same speed.

Displacement. Movement away from a fixed reference point.

Dock Leveler. A mechanical device that adjusts to accommodate the different heights of truck beds.

Dome. An arch rotated about a vertical axis passing through its crown, or highest point.

Door Solid Core. A door which has a core constructed with solid materials.

Dope Coat. Neat cement applied to the setting bed.

Double Bullnose. A type of trim with the same convex radius on two opposite sides.

Double Hung Window. The most common operable style of window. It has two sashes that slide vertically in parallel tracks.

Double Tee. A precast concrete slab element that resembles the letters "TT" in cross section.

Dovetail Joint. A joint which has a flaring tenon and a mortise into which it fits tightly and interlocks two pieces.

Dowel. A steel bar, which extends into two adjoining portions of a concrete construction, as at a joint in a pavement slab, so as to connect the portions and transfer shear loads. Also, as used in the construction of column and wall sections, a deformed steel reinforcing bar placed so as to transmit tension or compression as well as shear loads.

Dozer. A slang term used for a bulldozer.

Drag Strut. A structural member used to transfer lateral forces from one vertical element to another.

Dragline. A bucket attachment for a crane in a marsh or marine area, that digs soft, wet materials that must be excavated at some distance from the crane, and draws the bucket towards itself using a cable.

Drain Tile. Short-length sections of burned clay, concrete, etc., laid with open joints and surrounded with aggregate and covered with aphaltic paper or straw to drain the water from an area.

Drift. Lateral deflection of a building caused by wind or earthquake loads. The horizontal displacement or movement of structure when subjected to lateral forces. A discontinuity formed into the underside of a window sill or wall component to force adhering drops of water to fall free of the face of the building rather than move farther toward the interior. The projection of a window sill or water table to allow the water to drain clear of the side of the house below it.

Dry Pack. Concrete or mortar mixtures deposited and consolidated by dry packing. A low-slump grout tamped into the space in a connection between pre-cast concrete members, or between a steel column and the column base-plate.

Dry Set Tile. Tile set into an adhesive that seems dry but that adheres on contact.

Dry Well. A well, usually filled with gravel, to receive rain run-off water, in an area where the ground is not very permeable, for example, in areas of clay soil.

Drywall. An interior facing panel consisting of a gypsum core sandwiched between paper faces, also called gypsum board or plasterboard.

Duct Bus. A prefabricated unit containing one or more electric conductors, often a metal bar, that serves as a common connection for two or more circuits.

Ductile. The ability of a material to deform under tensile load.

Ductile Moment Resisting Space Frame. A three dimensional structural system without bearing walls and composed of interconnecting members that resists lateral forces with or without the aid of horizontal diaphragms.

Ductility. The quality of being able to deform considerably under load before fracturing. Contrasted to the quality of brittleness.

Dummy Joint. A joint placed strictly for design, in sidewalks and patios.

Dunting. The cracking that occurs in fired ceramic bodies due to thermally induced stresses.

DWV Pipe, ABS. A rigid plastic pipe manufactured from acrylonitrile butadiene styrene used as a drain, waste, or vent in a plumbing system.

Dynamic. Having to do with bodies in motion. Implying motion or change of state; opposite of Static (i.e.: an earthquake force is a dynamic force).

Dynamic Force. F=ma, or force equals mass times acceleration, a moving force.

Eagle Beak. A 6" x 3/4" outside corner trim shape tile.

Edge Bead. A strip of metal or plastic used to make a neat, durable edge where plaster or gypsum board abuts another material.

Edger. A finishing tool used on the edges of fresh concrete to provide a rounded corner.

Effective Stiffness. The value of the lateral force in the isolation system, or an element thereof, divided by the corresponding lateral displacement.

Efflorescence. A powdery deposit on the face of a structure of masonry or concrete, caused by the leaching of chemical salts by water migrating from within the structure to the surface.

Elastic. Able to return to its original size and shape after removed of stress.

Elasticity. Property of a material to deform under load and return to its original dimensions when load is removed.

Elastomeric Flashing. A rubber-like material used as flashing on a roof system.

Electrolysis. Production of chemical changes by the passage of current through an electrolyte.

Elevated Slab. A roof slab or floor supported by structural members.

EMT. Electrical Metallic Conduit - Thin Wall Conduit.

End Bell. Cast iron pipe with a wide opening at one end.

End Nail. A nail driven through one piece of lumber and into the end of another.

Energy Dissipation. Reduction in intensity of earthquake shock waves with time and distance.

Engineer. A person who uses the science by which the properties of matter and the sources of energy in nature are made useful to man.

English Bond. Brickwork laid with alternating courses, each consisting entirely of headers or stretchers.

Entrained Air. Microscopic air bubbles intentionally incorporated into mortar or concrete during mixing, usually by use of a surface-active agent, typically between 10 and 1,000 um in diameter and spherical or nearly so.

Epicenter. The point on the earth's surface vertically above the focus or hypocenter of an earthquake. The part of the earth's surface directly above the origin of an earthquake.

Epoxy Flooring. A resin spread on flooring to make a hard, tough surface.

Epoxy Grout. A two-part grout system consisting of epoxy resin and epoxy hardener, especially formulated to have impervious qualities, stain, and chemical resistance, used to fill joints between tile units.

Epoxy Mortar. A two-part mortar system consisting of epoxy resin and epoxy hardener used to bond tile to back-up material where chemical resistance of high bond strength is a consideration.

Equalizer. One that equalizes by distributing evenly or uniformly (as of force).

Equilibrium. A state of rest doe to balanced forces. State of being in balance; implies no tendency to change.

Equipment Pad. A thick slab-type stone or precast concrete block placed under mechanical devices to spread the weight and load of the machinery evenly and to prevent excessive vibration.

Equivalent Static Force Analysis. A method by which a dynamic force is translated into an equivalent static force that produces a similar effect.

Ergonomics. Applied science that investigates the impact of people's physical environment on their health and comfort (e.g., determining the proper chair height for computer operators).

Evaporative Condenser. Hot gas discharged from the compressor is piped to the condenser coil within the casing of the outdoor evaporation condenser. Water is sprayed directly onto the coil where it encounters an air stream causing some of the water to evaporate.

Exhaust Fan. An electrical powered device to withdraw fumes, dusts, or odors from an enclosure.

Exit Light. A light assembly over an exit door that is independently powered to remain lit in the event of a catastrophe, to guide persons to safety.

Expansion Joint. A joint through tile, mortar, and reinforcing wire down to the substrate. A discontinuity intended to allow for gross movement due to thermal stress, or material shrinkage.

Exposed Aggregate Finish. A concrete surface in which the coarse aggregate is revealed.

Extrusion. The process of squeezing a material through a shaped orifice to produce a linear element with the desired cross section; an element produced by this process.

Facade. An exterior face of a building.

Face Brick. A brick selected on the basis of appearance and durability for use in the exposed surface of a wall.

Factored Load. The load imposed on a member multiplied by appropriate factors, used to design reinforced concrete members by the strength design method.

Fan Coil Unit (FCU). A packaged unit consisting of a heating/cooling coil, fan, and filter, without ductwork, used to serve a space or a group of small spaced.

Fascia. A flat member or band at the surface of a building or the edge beam of a bridge; exposed eaves of a building; often inappropriately called facia.

Fatigue. A structural failure which occurs as the result of a load being applied and removed, or reversed, repeatedly over a long period of time, or a large number of cycles.

Fault. A break in the continuity of a rock formation which is caused by the shifting of the earth's crust.

Feather Edge. A wood or metal tool having a beveled edge; used to straighten re-entrant angles in finish plaster coat; also edge of a concrete or mortar placement such as a patch or topping that is beveled at an acute angle.

Feeder Duct. An enclosure for a group of electrical conductors that runs power from a central, large source to one or more secondary distribution centers.

Fiberboard. A homogeneous panel made from wood or cane fibers.

Fiberglass. The name for products made of or with glass fibers ranging from 5 to 600 hundred-thousandths inch in diameter. Used for making textile fabrics, and for heat or sound insulation.

Field Tile. An area of tile covering a wall or floor. The field is bordered by tile trim.

Fillet Weld. A weld at the inside intersection of two metal surfaces that meet at right angles.

Finger Joint. A glued end connection between two pieces of wood, using an interlocking pattern of deeply cut "fingers". A finger joint creates a large surface for the glue bond, to allow it to develop the full tensile strength of the wood it connects.

Finish. The final work on a construction job.

Fire Damper. A damper that automatically closes a duct upon detection of fire.

Fire Detection Annunciator. A mechanical device which audibly announces a warning in case of a fire.

Fire Door. A door which has been manufactured with specific materials to help hold back the spread of fire.

Fire Resistance Rating. The time, in hours, or fractions of an hour, that a material or assembly will resist fire exposure as determined by ASTM E119.

Fire Wall. A wall, required under the building code, which divides two parts of a building, to serve as a deterrent to the spread of fire.

Firestop. A wood baffle used to close an opening between studs or joists in a balloon or platform frame in order to retard the spread of fire through the opening.

Flame Spread Rating. A measure of the rapidity with which fire will spread across the surface of a material as determined by ASTM E84.

Flashing. A thin, continuous sheet of metal, plastic, rubber or waterproof paper used to prevent the passage of water through a joint in a wall, roof or chimney. The material used and the process of making watertight the roof intersections and other exposed places on the outside of the house.

Flemish Bond. Brickwork laid with each course consisting of alternating headers and stretchers.

Flexible Conduit. Metallic conduit that is flexible and is put up in coils instead of lengths. May be used in lieu of the rigid type in most dry locations.

Flexural Strength. A property of a material or structural member that indicates its ability to resist failure in bedding.

Float. A tool or apparatus for smoothing a surface.

Float Finish. A finish coat that is rough from aggregate material found in the plaster mortar.

Float Strip. A strip of wood about 1/4" thick and 1-1/4" wide. It is used as a guide to align mortar surfaces.

Floating. A method of using a straightedge to align mortar with the float strips or screeds. This technique also is called dragging, pulling, rodding, or rodding off.

Floor, Access. A raised floor platform with removable panels to provide access to an area below.

Floor Joist. A common support beam.

Flue. A passage for smoke and combustion products from a furnace, stove, water heater or fireplace.

Fluted Column. Columns with decorative, semi-circular channeled shafts.

Footing. The widened part of a foundation that spreads a load from the building across a broader area of soil. An enlargement at the lower end of a wall, pier, or column, to distribute the load.

Force. Energy exerted on an element tending to cause motion. Magnitude, direction and point of application are all used to describe a force.

Form Oil. Oil applied to interior surface of formwork to promote easy release from the concrete when forms are removed.

Form Tie. A steel rod with fasteners on each end, used to hold together the formwork for a concrete wall.

Formboard. A formwork board or sheet of wood.

Foundation Backfill. Earth or earthen material displaced during excavation and replaced around the constructed foundation.

Foundation Investigation (soil report). A geological report from a geological engineer providing information on the subsurface soil conditions.

Fracture. A break, usually resulting in actual separation of the material. In structures, the characteristic result of tension failure.

Frame, Ductile Moment Resisting. A frame which is capable of resisting bending moments in the joints, enabling it to resist lateral forces or unsymmetrical vertical loads through bending action of the frame. Stability is achieved through bending action rather than bracing.

Frame, Moment. A structural frame which is capable of transferring bending moments through connections, enabling it to resist lateral forces or unsymmetrical vertical loads through overall bending action of the frame.

Framing. The rough timber structure of a building, including interior and exterior walls, floor, roof, and ceilings.

Friction Connection. Two or more structural steel members clamped together by high-strength bolts with sufficient force that the loads on the members are transmitted between them by friction along their mating surfaces.

Friction Piling. A load-bearing pile that has its supporting capacity from the skin friction between the soil in contact with the pile.

Front-End Loader. A tractor or bulldozer with a bucket which operates only at the front.

Furring. Stripping used to build out a surface such as a studded wall where strips of suitable size are added to the studs to accommodate vent pipes or other fixtures. Narrow strips of board nailed upon the walls and ceilings to form a straight surface upon which to lay the lath or other finish.

Fuse. An overcurrent protection device.

Fusion. The process of melting; usually the result of interaction of two or more materials.

Gabion. An iron cylinder filled with earth used in mining.

Gable. The triangular wall beneath the end of a gable roof.

Gable. The vertical triangular end of a building from the eaves to the apex of the roof.

Gable Roof. A roof consisting of two opposite sloping planes that intersect at a level ridge.

Gable-End Rafter. The last rafter system installed at the gable end of a building.

Galvanized. Zinc plating for corrosion protection by hot dipping into molten zinc or by electrolysis.

Gang Box. Electrical boxes constructed of metal or hard plastic, manufactured with knockout holes to pull wire through to connect outlets and switches.

Gate Valve. A valve utilizing a wedge-shaped gate, which allows fluid flow when the gate is lifted from the seat.

General Conditions. A written document, supplementing the specifications, which indicates and defines specific areas of the project.

Girt. A beam that supports wall cladding between columns.

Girt (ribband). The horizontal member of the walls of a full or combination frame house which supports the floor joists or is flush with the top of the joists.

Glaze. A ceramic coating matured to the glassy state on a formed ceramic article. The term glaze also refers to the material or mixture from which the coating is made.

Glazing. The act or process of furnishing or fitting with glass. A transparent or translucent color applied to modify the effect of a painted surface.

Globe Valve. A valve with a rounded disc that shuts off the flow when closed, and seats to prevent fluid flow.

Glue Built-up Members. Structural elements, the sections of which are composed of built-up lumber, wood structural panels or wood structural panels in combination with lumber, all parts bonded together with adhesives.

Glue Joint. A joint held together with glue.

Glue-Laminated Beam. An engineered, stress-rated, product assembled of especially selected and prepared wood laminations that are securely bonded together with adhesives.

Glulam. An abbreviation of glue laminated timber.

Graben (rift valley). A long, narrow trough bounded by one or more parallel normal faults.

Grade. The horizontal ground level of a building or structure.

Grade Beam. A reinforced concrete beam that transmits the load from a bearing wall into spaced foundations such as pile caps or caissons.

Granular Insulation. Insulating material made of granular vermiculite or perlite or beaded styrene, placed in hollow (usually masonry) construction.

Gravel. Rock particles retained on a No. 4 sieve that result from natural disintegration or are processed from weakly bound conglomerate.

Gravel Stop. A metal flange or strip with a vertical lip placed around a built-up roof to prevent loose gravel from falling off the roof.

Gravity Wall. A retaining wall which depends solely on its weight to resist lateral forces of retained earth.

Ground Acceleration. Acceleration of the ground due to earthquake forces.

Ground Bus. In the main electrical service panel, where the neutral service wire (generally white) attaches and is linked to the earth by the ground wire.

Ground Fault Circuit Interrupter (GFCI). Supplies power, as any receptacle does, but also monitors the amount of incoming and outgoing current. Whenever the entering current does not equal the leaving current, indicating current leakage, the GFCI instantly opens the circuit.

Grout. A rich or strong cementitious or chemically setting mix used for filling tile joints. A mixture of portland cement, aggregates, and water, which can be poured or pumped into cavities in concrete or masonry.

Gunite. A term used to describe a concrete material applied by pumping through a hose.

Gusset Plate. A flat steel plate to which the chords are connected at a joint in a truss; a stiffener plate.

Guy Cable. Cable anchored at one end and supporting or stabilizing an object at other end.

Guy Rod. A metal rod with a cable or rope attached, leading to an object to support and stabilize it.

Gypsum. Hydrous calcium sulfate.

Gypsum Board. An interior facing panel consisting of a gypsum core sandwiched between paper faces. Also called drywall or plasterboard.

Gypsum Lath. Small sheets of gypsum board manufactured specifically for use as a plaster base.

Hairline Cracking. Small cracks of random pattern in an exposed concrete surface.

Handicapped Plumbing. Plumbing devices and layouts specifically designed for use by disabled persons.

Hanger. Vertical-tension member supporting a load.

Hanger Joist. A metal stirrup that supports the ends of joists so that they are flush with the girder.

Hard Screed. A mortar screed that has become firm.

Hardboard. A very dense panel product, usually with at least one smooth face, made of highly compressed wood fibers.

Hardware. A general term for metal or plastic fittings used in or on a building and its parts

Hatch. A hinged or removable cover in a floor or roof, which permits ventilation or the passage of persons or objects.

Head Joint. The vertical layer of mortar between ends of masonry units.

Header. Lintel; a joist that supports other joists; in steel construction, a beam that spans between girders.

Headwall. A wall, usually constructed of concrete or masonry, that is placed at the outlet side of a drain or culvert to protect fill from scouring, undermining or to divert flow.

Heat Pump. A unit that supplies heating or cooling to an interior space by either absorbing heat from or rejecting heat to the outside; a unit utilizing the vapor compression refrigeration cycle in the same way a Dx unit or chiller does.

Hertz (Hz). A measurement of the frequency of vibration of sound measured in cycles per second. One cycle per seconds equal one Hertz (Hz).

Hex Nut. A six-sided, short metal nut with a threaded hole for receiving a rod or threaded bolt.

High Chair Reinforcing. A slang term describing a chair-shaped device used to hold steel reinforcement off of the slab.

High-lift Grouting. A method of construction in which concrete block units may be laid the entire height of the wall before grouting. This method of construction requires special inspection.

Hip. The diagonal intersection of planes in a hip roof.

Hip Roof. A roof consisting of four sloping planes that intersect to form a pyramidal or elongated pyramid shape. A roof which slopes up toward the center from all sides, necessitating a hip rafter at each corner.

Hod. A portable trough for carrying mortar, bricks, etc., fixed crosswise on top of a pole and carried on the shoulder.

Hollow Core Slab. A precast concrete slab element that has internal longitudinal cavities to reduce its self-weight.

Hose Bibb. An outdoor water faucet, usually at sill height, used as a hose connection.

Hot Mud or Hot Stuff. Mortar mixed with an accelerator.

Humidity. The amount of water vapor in a given space.

Hung Slab. A nonstructural concrete slab having no bearing on walls, being totally supported from above by an overhead structural element.

HVAC. Heating, ventilation, and air-conditioning system.

Hydrant. A connection to a water main used for the dispensation of water.

Hydrate. A chemical combination of water with another compound or an element.

Hydronic Heating System. A system that circulates warm water through convectors to heat a building.

Hydrostatic Pressure. Pressure exerted by standing water.

Hyperbolic Paraboloid. Double curved surface which can be generated by sliding a straight line along two other lines which are skew to each other but lie in parallel planes.

Hyperbolic paraboloid shell. A concrete roof structure with a saddle shape.

Hypocenter. The point below the epicenter at which an earthquake actually begins; the focus.

I. Represents the moment of inertia of a member.

I-Beam. An obsolete term; an American Standard designation for a section of hot-rolled steel.

ICBO. International Conference of Building Officials, 5360 South Workman Mill Road, Whittier, California 90601, (310) 699-0451.

Ice Dam. An obstruction along the eaves of a roof caused by the refreezing of water emanating from melting snow on the roof surface above.

Indirect Luminaire. A lighting fixture that distributes most of its light upward.

Inelastic Behavior. Behavior of an element beyond its elastic limit.

Instruction To Bidders. More informative information given to identified bidders than included in the invitation to bid.

Insulation. Any material used to reduce the effects of heat, cold or sound and to reduce fire hazard. Any material used in the prevention of the transfer of electricity, heat, cold, moisture and sound.

Interceptors. A device that collects foreign matter and prevents it from reaching the public sewer system.

Invert Manhole. The lowest inside surface of a manhole.

Inverted Roof. A membrane roof assembly in which the thermal insulation lies above the membrane.

Isolation Joint. A separation between adjoining parts of a concrete structure, usually a vertical plane, at a designed location such as to interfere least with performance of the structure, yet such as to allow relative movement and avoid formation of cracks elsewhere in the concrete and through which all or part of the bonded reinforcement is interrupted.

Jack Rafter. A short rafter framing between the wall plate; a hip rafter.

Jalousie Window. A window with stationary or adjustable blinds angled to permit air and provide shade, while at the same time preventing rain from entering.

Jamb. The vertical side of a door or window. The side piece or post of an opening; sometimes applied to the door frame.

Jitterbug. A grate tamper for pushing coarse aggregate slightly below the surface of a slab to facilitate finishing.

Job Built Form. A temporary structure or mold constructed on a jobsite, for the support of concrete while it is setting and gaining sufficient strength to be self-supporting.

Joint. The point of connection between structural members.

Joint Clip. A fastener used vertically, sharp edge down, over the joining edges of two pieces, and then hammered down into them.

Joint Expansion. A discontinuity intended to allow for gross movement to thermal stress, or material shrinkage.

Joist Hanger. A metal stirrup that supports the ends of joists so that they are flush with the girder.

Joist Sister. The reinforcement of a joist by nailing or attaching a stronger piece to a weaker one.

Joists. Timbers supporting the floorboards.

Joule. In the international system of units, the amount of energy needed to raise 1 kilogram of water 1 degree Celsius.

Journeyman. An experienced reliable worker who has learned his trade and works for another person.

Junction Box. A metal box in which runs of cable are protectively enclosed.

K Bracing. That form of bracing where a pair of braces located on one side of a column terminates at a single point within the clear column height.

Keene's Cement. A cement composed of finely ground, anhydrous, calcined gypsum, the set of which is accelerated by the addition of other materials.

Kelly Ball Test. A method by which the workability of fresh concrete can be determined.

Key. A slot formed into a concrete surface for the purpose of interlocking with a subsequent pour of concrete; a slot at the edge of a precast member into which grout will be poured to lock it to an adjacent member.

Kick Plate. A metal plate or strip that runs along the bottom edge of a door to protect against the marring of the finish.

Kiln Dried. Lumber that has been heated in a kiln to control amounts of moisture.

King Post Truss. In a roof system, the member placed vertically between the center of the horizontal tie beam at the lower end of the rafters and the ridge, or apex of the inclined rafters.

Kip. A unit of weight or force equal to 1,000 lbs.

Knee Brace. A corner brace, fastened at an angle from wall stud to rafter, stiffening a wood or steel frame to prevent angular movement.

Knee Wall. A short wall under the slope of a roof.

Labor and Material Bond. A bond, secured by the general contractor, which guarantees that the labor and materials for the project will be paid for.

Lag Rod. A large diameter rod with a square or hexagonal head.

Lag Screw. A large diameter wood screw with a square or hexagonal head.

Laitance. A layer of weak and nondurable material containing cement and fines from aggregates, brought by bleeding water to the top of overwet concrete, the amount of which is generally increased by overworking or over manipulating concrete at the surface by improper finishing or by job traffic.

Lateral. From the side - horizontal; wind and earthquake are considered lateral forces.

Lateral Load. The horizontal component of the force produced by an arch, dome, vault, or rigid frame. A horizontal load applied to a structure or member such as wind or earthquake.

Lateral Thrust. The horizontal component of the force produced by an arch, dome, vault, or rigid frame.

Lateral-Force-Resisting System. That portion of the structure composed of members proportioned to resist forces related to earthquake effects.

Lath. A wood strip or metal mesh, which acts as a background or reinforcing agent for the scratch coat or mortar coat.

Lattice. Crossed wood, iron plate, or bars.

Layout Stick. A long strip of wood marked at the appropriate joint intervals for the tile to be used. It is used to check the length, width, or height of the tilework. A common name for this item is idiot stick.

Leaching Pit. A pit that can hold solids put allows liquids to pass through.

Ledgerboard. The support for the second-floor joists of a balloon-frame house, or for similar uses; ribband.

Leveling Plate. A steel plate placed in grout on top of a concrete foundation to crease a level bearing surface for the lower end of a steel column.

LH Joist. Left hand, long-span, high strength bar joist.

Lift-Slab Construction. A method of building multistory sitecast concrete buildings by casting all the slabs in a stack on the ground, then lifting them up the columns with jacks and welding them in place.

Lightning Arrester. A device that protects electrical units from lightning and power surges.

Lintel. The horizontal beam placed over an opening.

Liquefaction. Transformation of a granular material (soil) from a solid state into a liquefied state as a consequence of vibrations induced by an earthquake.

Live Load. The weight of people, furnishings, machines, and goods in or on a building. The vertical load superimposed by the use and occupancy of a building.

Load. A force that is applied to a body. A weight or force acting on a structure. Applied external force, such as gravity and wind.

Load Bearing. Supporting a superimposed weight or force.

Load, Factored. The load, multiplied by appropriate load factors, used to proportion members by the strength design method of this code.

Load-Bearing Wall. A wall designed and built to carry superimposed vertical and shear loads as opposed to nonload-bearing walls.

Lockset. A device installed in a door that has both a deadbolt and doorknob assembly.

Lookout. The end of a rafter, or the construction which projects beyond the sides of a house to support the eaves; also the projecting timbers at the gables which support the verge boards.

Louver. A construction of numerous sloping, closely spaced slats used to prevent the entry of rain or snow into a ventilating opening. A kind of window, generally in peaks of gables and the tops of towers, provided with horizontal slots which exclude rain and snow and allow ventilation.

Low-Lift Grouting. A method of constructing a reinforced masonry wall in which the wall is grouted in increments not higher than 4 feet.

Lumber. Wood members which are manufactured by sawing, resawing, passing lengthwise through standard planing machine, crosscutting to length, and matching, but without further manufacturing.

Lumen. A quantitative unit for the measurement of the flow of light energy.

Make-Up Air. Air brought into a building from outdoors through the ventilation system and that has not been previously circulated through the system.

Malleable Iron. Iron that can be hammered or bent without breaking.

Manhole. A hole through which a person may go to gain access to an underground or enclosed structure.

Manhole Watertight. A cover for a vertical access shaft that prevents the outside elements in.

Mansard. A roof shape consisting of two superimposed levels of hip roofs with the lower level at a steeper pitch.

Mantle. The main bulk of the earth between the crust and core, varying in depth from 40 to 3,480 kilometers.

Masonry. Brickwork, blockwork, and stonework.

Masonry Reinforcing. Lateral steel rods or mesh placed between courses of masonry units.

Mass. The property of an object that causes it to resist changes in its state of motion. This resistance is called inertia.

Mastic. A viscous, dough-like, adhesive substance; can be any of a large number of formulations for different purposes such as sealants, adhesives, glazing compounds, or roofing membranes.

Maximum Capable Earthquake. The maximum level of earthquake ground shaking which may ever be expected at the building site within the known geological framework. (In Seismic Zones 3 and 4), this intensity may be taken as the level of earthquake ground motion that has a 10 percent probability of being exceeded in a 100-year time period.

Mean Radiant Temperature. The weighted average of all radiating surface temperatures within one line of sight.

Mercury Fixture. A light fixture that has an electric discharge lamp that produces a blue-white light by creating an arc in mercury vapor enclosed in a tube or globe.

Mercury Switch. An electrical switch that has mercury enclosed in a vial to make a silent contact.

Mesh Slab. Welded-wire fabric in sheets or rolls to reinforce concrete slabs.

Millwork. All building materials, such as doors and windows, but not including floors, sidings and ceilings, made of wood produced in a planing mill.

Miter. The joint formed by two abutting pieces meeting at an angle.

Mixer, Colloidal. a mixer designed to produce colloidal grout.

Mixing Water. The water in freshly mixed sand-cement grout, mortar, or concrete, exclusive of any previously absorbed by the aggregate (e.g., water considered in the computation of the net water-cement ratio.)

Modulus of Deformation. A concept of modulus of elasticity expressed as a function of two time variables; strain in loaded concrete as a function of the age at which the load is initially applied and of the length of time the load is sustained.

Moisture Barrier. A membrane used to prevent the migration of liquid water through a floor or wall.

Molding. A strip of wood, plastic or plaster with an ornamental profile.

Molding Plaster. A fast-setting gypsum plaster used for the manufacture of cast ornament.

Moment. A force acting at a distance from a point in a structure so as to cause a tendency of the structure to rotate about that point. The act of a force to cause rotation about a given point or axis.

Moment Connection. A connection between two structural members that is highly resistant to rotation between the members, as differentiated from a pin connection, which allow rotation.

Moment Distribution. A method of structural analysis for continuous beams and rigid frames whereby successive converging corrections are made to an assumed set of moments until the desired precision is obtained; also known as the Hardy Cross method.

Moment Resisting Frame. A frame composed of rigid joints in which the members and joints resist both vertical and horizontal forces.

Moment, Positive. By usual sign convention, a beam which is bent downward (sagging), is considered to be subjected to positive bending.

Monolith. A body of plain or reinforced concrete cast or erected as a single integral mass or structure.

Monolithic Concrete. Concrete cast with no joints or as one piece.

Mortar. A mixture of cement paste and fine aggregate; in fresh concrete, the material occupying the interstices among particles of coarse aggregate; in masonry construction, mortar may contain masonry cement, or may contain hydraulic cement with lime (and possibly other admixtures) to afford greater plasticity and workability than are attainable with standard hydraulic cement mortar.

Mortarboard. The mortarboard is used as a table to hold mortar. It is usually 30" square.

Mortise. The hole which is to receive a tenon, or any hole cut into or through a piece by a chisel; generally of rectangular shape.

Mortise-and-Tenon. A join in which a tongue-like protrusion (tenon) on the end of one piece is tightly fitted into a rectangular slot (mortise) in the side of the other piece.

Mortised Joint. A joint made by cutting a hole or mortise, in one piece, and a tenon, or piece to fit the hole, upon the other.

Mud. A slang term for mortar.

Mullion. A vertical or horizontal bar between adjacent window or door units.

Muntin. The vertical member between two panels of the same piece of panel work. The vertical sash-bars separating the different panels of glass.

Natural Convection. Fluid motion of air caused by the temperature difference between the solid surface and the fluid with which it is in contact.

Natural Frequency. The constant frequency of a vibrating system in the state of natural oscillation.

Neat Cement. Hydraulic cement in the unhydrated state.

Needle Beam. A steel or wood beam threaded through a hole in a bearing wall and used to support the wall and its superimposed loads during underpinning of its foundation.

Negative Pressure. Condition that exists when less air is supplied to a space than is exhausted from the space, so the air pressure within that space is less than that in surrounding areas.

Neoprene. A type of synthetic rubber with outstanding oil resistance. Can be used for quick-setting, high strength adhesives.

Neutral Axis. The line on a member cross-section on which the bending moment is zero.

Nominal Size (Lumber). The commercial size designation of width and depth, in standard sawn lumber and glued-laminated lumber grades; larger than the standard net size of dressed lumber.

Nonaxial. In a direction not parallel to the long axis of a structural member.

Nonbearing. Not carrying a load.

Nosing. The projecting forward edge of a stair tread. The part of a stair tread which projects over the riser, or any similar projection; a term applied to the rounded edge of a board.

Notice of Completion. A written document, filed with the county in which the project is located, verifying that the project is complete and ready for occupancy. This document initiates the beginning of the last 30 days of the lien period.

Oil Switch. A switch or protector relay installed in a flue pipe, that will shut off a burner in case the stack does not come up to a predetermined temperature within 45 seconds after the motor starts.

Ornamental Metal. A detail that is added to a building constructed of metal, with the purpose of embellishment.

Outrigger Flagpole. A projecting pole run out from a main structure to provide additional stability or to support an extension.

Overhang Beam. A beam that is supported by two or more supports and has one or both ends projecting beyond the support.

P-Trap. A P-shaped device that prevents sewer air from escaping from a plumbing fixture, such as a sink.

Pad Bearing. A thick slab-type stone or precast concrete block placed under a structural member of a building to spread the load or weight evenly.

Panic Hardware. A mechanical device that opens a door automatically if pressure is exerted against the device from the interior of the building.

Paper and Wire. Tar paper and wire mesh (or metal lath) that are used as a backing for the installation of tile.

Paper Building. A generic term for felts, papers and sheet materials used in building applications.

Parapet. The region of an exterior wall that projects above the level of the roof.

Parging. Portland cement plaster applied over masonry to make it less permeable to water.

Parquet Floor. A floor covering laid out in a geometric design composed of small pieces of wood.

Particle Board. A building panel composed of small particles of wood bonded together under pressure.

Paver. A half-thickness brick used as finish flooring.

Paver, Stone. Blocks of rock processed by shaping, cutting or sizing, used for driveways and patios.

Pea Gravel. Screened gravel particles most of which would pass through a 3/8 inch (9.5mm) sieve.

Pedestal. A short compression member of reinforced concrete that is placed between a column and the footing to distribute the load to the footing.

Performance Bond. A bond, secured by the general contractor, which guarantees that the contract will be performed.

Perlite. Expanded volcanic rock, used as a lightweight aggregate in concrete and plaster, and as an insulating fill.

Photovoltaic. A process of conversion of sunlight into electricity.

Pier. Timber, concrete, or masonry supports for girders, posts, or arches. Intermediate supports for adjacent ends of two bridge spans. Structure extending outward from shore into water used as a dock for ship. Masonry supports, set independently of the main foundation.

Pilaster. A vertical, integral stiffening rib in a masonry or concrete wall.

Pile. A long, slender, piece of material driven into the ground to act as a foundation. A member embedded into the ground that supports vertical loads. Can be made of wood, steel or concrete.

Pile Cap. A thick slab of reinforced concrete poured across the top of a pile group to cause the group to act as a unit in supporting a column.

Pipe Cleanout. A pipe fitting placed in a drain waste (DWV) system in each horizontal section of drain for removing blockages.

Pipe, PVC. Polyvinyl chloride pipe used mainly for drain lines and is particularly resistant to chemicals.

Plaster. A cementitious material, usually based on gypsum or portland cement, which is applied to lath or masonry in paste form, to harden into a finish surface. A mixture of lime, hair, and sand, or of lime, cement, and sand, used to cover outside and inside wall surfaces.

Plaster of Paris. Pure calcined gypsum.

Plasterboard. A board used in large sheets as a backing or as a substitute for plaster in walls and consisting of fiberboard, paper, or felt, bonded to a hardened gypsum plaster core.

Plastic. In stress analysis, refers to stress/strain behavior beyond the elastic range. Plastic deformation usually implies some permanent shape change.

Plastic Laminate. Sheet material manufactured of multiple layers of paper with top layer of plastic usually 1/16 inch (1.59 mm) thick with decorative finish. Used to finish cabinets and casework. Plastic laminate may be used in flat sheets or heat formed bent, and adhered to single curved base material.

Plasticity. Property of a material to deform under load and to retain the deformation after the load is removed; usually implies that stress is not directly proportional to strain.

Plate. The top horizontal piece of the walls of a frame building upon which the roof rests.

Plate, Armor. A metal plate that is mounted usually not less than 36 inches high on the lower part of a door, to protect it from kicks and scratches.

Plate Cut. The cut in a rafter which rests upon the plate; sometimes called the seat cut.

Plate Girder. A large beam made up of steel plates, sometimes in combination with steel angles, welded, bolted or revitted together.

Plate Glass. Glass of high optical quality produced by grinding and polishing both faces of a glass sheet.

Platform. Horizontal surface occurring in stair at end of flight or between flights, either at floor level or between floors.

Plenum. Air compartment connected to a duct or ducts.

Plumb. Vertical, or perfectly straight up and down.

Plumb Cut. Any cut made in a vertical plane; the vertical cut at the top end of a rafter.

Plumbing. The act or process of installing in a building or structure the pipes, fixtures, or other apparatus for bringing in the water supply and removing liquid and water-borne wastes. The installed fixtures and piping of a building or structure.

Ply. A term used to denote a layer or thickness of building or roofing paper as two-ply, three-ply, etc.

Plywood. A wood panel composed of a number of layers of wood veneer bonded and glued together under pressure.

Plywood Shear Wall. Wall constructed of studs and plywood sheathing that in its own plane resists shear forces resulting from applied wind, earthquake or other transverse loads or provides frame stability.

Pneumatic System. Mechanical devices powered by compressed air.

Pointing Masonry. The act or process of applying mortar to a masonry surface joint after masonry has been laid, either as a means of finishing the joint or to repair a defective joint.

Porch. An ornamental entrance way.

Portland Cement. The element used as the binder in concrete, mortar, and stucco.

Post. A timber set on end to support a wall, girder, or other member of the structure.

Pour. To cast concrete; an increment of concrete casting carried out without interruption.

Precast. Concrete slabs, reinforced lintels, beams, columns and parts of walls and floors that are cast and cured in other than their final position.

Precast Concrete. Concrete cast and cured in a position other than its final position in the structure.

Prehung Door. A door that is hinged to its frame in a factory or shop.

Pressure Regulators. Automatic valves located between a compressor and evaporator outlet that is responsive to its own inlet pressure or to the evaporator or refrigerator temperature. It throttles the vapor flow when necessary to prevent the evaporator pressure from falling below a selected value.

Pressure-Treated Lumber. Lumber that has been impregnated with chemicals under pressure, for the purpose of retarding either decay or fire.

Prestressed Concrete. Concrete that has been pretensioned or post-tensioned.

Pretensioning. A method by which the design tensile force is applied to the steel reinforcing before the concrete is set.

Prism. An assemblage of masonry units and mortar with or without grout used as a test specimen for determining properties of the masonry.

Projecting Sash. A window with sashes that swing either inward or outward.

Proposal. The document submitted by the contractor to the owner for construction of the project, sometimes called "the bid".

Psychrometrics. A branch of physics dealing with the study of atmospheric conditions, specifically the relationships between moisture and air.

Pump, Sump. A small capacity pump that empties pits receiving sewage or liquid waste.

Purger, Air. A mechanical device that removes unwanted air by injecting an inert gas into a ductline, pipeline, container, space, or furnace.

Purlin. A timber supporting several rafters at one or more points, or the roof sheeting directly.

PVC Pipe. Polyvinyl chloride pipe used mainly for drain lines and is particularly resistant to chemicals.

Quarry Tile. A large clay floor tile, usually unglazed.

R-value. The number of minutes (seconds) required for 1 Btu (joule) to penetrate one square foot (square meter) of a material for each degree of temperature difference between the two sides of the material. The resistance of a material to the passage of heat. The reciprocal of conductors (1/c).

Rabbet. A corner cut out of an edge of a piece of wood.

Raceway. Any channel supporting and protecting electrical conductors, including conduits, wireways, surface metal raceway, cable trays, floor and ceiling raceways, busways and cable bus.

Rafter. A framing member that runs up and down the slope of a pitched roof. The beams that slope from the ridge of a roof to the eaves and make up the main body of the roof's framework.

Rafters, Common. Those which run square with the plate and extend to the ridge.

Rail. The horizontal members of the balustrade or panel work.

Rake. The sloping edge of a pitched roof. The trim of a building extending in an oblique line, as rake dado or molding.

Ranch Casing. An architectural style of exposed millwork enclosure of cased beams, posts, pipes, etc. and the exposed molding or lining around doors and windows.

Rapid Start Lamp. A lamp operated by a ballast that provides a low-voltage winding to preheat electrodes and initiate the arc without a starting switch or the application of high voltage.

Re-Entrainment. Situation that occurs when the air being exhausted from a building is immediately brought back into the system through the air intake and other openings in the building envelope.

Receptacle, Combination. An electrical fixture with an outlet for plugging in an electric appliance, along with an electric switch for operating another circuit.

Recessed Light Fixture. A light fixture installed in a suspended ceiling or a recess in a plaster ceiling.

Reciprocating Chiller. A compressor (single-acting) using pistons that are driven by a connecting rod from a crankshaft.

Record Drawings (As Built). A set of drawings prepared by the general contractor, which includes any revisions in the working drawings and specifications during construction, indicating how the project was actually constructed.

Recording Voltmeter. A device which records the continuity, power, grounding, voltage and resistance of electrical circuits.

Reducer. A trim unit used to reduce the radius of a bullnose or a cove to another radius or to a square.

Reducer, Copper. A pipe fitting which connects pipes of different sizes, manufactured from copper.

Reducer, Fuse. The act or process of welding a pipe coupling with one larger end than the other to a length of pipe.

Refraction. The bending of a light ray as it passes obliquely through a material.

Refractories. Heat-resistant non-metallic ceramic materials.

Refractory, Concrete. Concrete having refractory properties, and suitable for use at high temperatures (generally about 315 to 1315 C), in which the binding agent is a hydraulic cement.

Register. An opening to a room or space with a grille and a damper that forms the end of ductwork for the passage of conditioned air. The wall upon which the grille and damper are installed that forms the end of ductwork for the passage of conditioned air.

Reglet. A flat, narrow architectural molding.

Reglet Roof. A roof which has a flat, narrow architectural molding.

Reinforced Concrete. Concrete work into which steel bars have been embedded to impart tensile strength to the construction.

Reinforcement, Mesh. Welded-wire fabric and Welded-wire fabric reinforcement. Heavy wires, welded together and used as reinforcing mostly for slabs.

Relative Humidity. The ratio of the quantity of water vapor actually present to amount present in a saturated atmosphere at a given temperature; expressed as a percentage. The ratio of the actual vapor pressure of the air-vapor pressure to the pressure of saturated water vapor at the same dry-bulb temperature times 100..

Relief Valve. A pressure-activated valve which allows air or fluid to escape if its pressure becomes more excessive than the valve setting.

Resilience. The measurement of the absorption of dynamic energy by a structure without permanent deformation or fracture.

Resolving Forces. Replacing a force or forces with two or more other forces that yield the same effect on a structure as the original forces.

Resonance. Movement produced in an element as a result of movement added to its natural period of movement, which is the same.

Resultant. A force that will produce the same effect as two or more forces.

Retaining Wall. A wall that is designed to resist the lateral pressures of retained soil.

Return. The ending of a small splash wall or a wainscot at right angle to the major wall. The continuation of a molding or finish of any kind in a different direction.

Richter Scale. A logarithmic scale that is used to measure the magnitude of earthquakes.

Rigid Frame. Two columns and a beam or beams attached with moment connections; a moment-resisting building frame. The connections between the beam and columns are constructed so as to transmit moments.

Rigidity. Relative stiffness of a structure or element.

Riprap. A foundation or sustaining wall of stones placed together without order (as in deep water or on an embankment slope to prevent erosion).

Rise. The vertical distance through which anything rises, as the rise of a roof or stair.

Riser. A single vertical increment of a stair; the vertical face between two treads in a stair; a vertical run of plumbing, wiring or ductwork.

Riser Hanger. The horizontal member of a stair structure which supports the riser.

Rock Anchor. A post-tensioned rod or cable inserted into a rock formation for the purpose of tying it together.

Rock Caisson. A drilled, cylindrical foundation shaft filled with rock.

Rod Hanger. A rod for connecting pipe, gutters, or ceiling framework to a support.

Roof Bond. A legal guarantee that a roof installed is in accordance with specifications and will be repaired or replaced if it fails in a certain period of time due to normal weathering.

Room Resonance. The resonance of an enclosed space with reflective material, which depends in the relationship between the sound wavelength and the space dimensions.

Rowlock. A brick laid on its long edge, with its end exposed in the face of the wall.

Run. Horizontal dimension in a stair. The length of the horizontal projection of a piece such as a rafter when in position.

Running Bond. Brickwork consisting entirely of stretchers.

Rusticated Concrete. Beveled edges of concrete making the joints conspicuous.

Sabin. The unit of acoustic absorption. One sabin is the absorption of one square foot of perfect sound-absorbing material.

Safety Nosing. Stair nosing with abrasive non-slip surface flush with tread surface.

Safety Tread. Stair tread which is covered on top surface with abrasive or non-slip material.

Safing. Fire-resistant material inserted into a space between a curtain wall and a spandrel beam or column, to retard the passage of fire through the space.

Sag Pond. A pond occupying depression along a fault. The depression is normally due to uneven settling of the ground or other causes.

Salamander. A portable source of heat, customarily oil-burning, used to heat an enclosure around or over newly placed concrete to prevent the concrete from freezing.

Samples. Material samples requested by the architect of the general contractor or materials specified for the project.

Sandblasting. A method of scarifying the surface of concrete or masonry to provide a bondable surface. Compressed air is used to propel a stream of wet or dry sand onto the surface.

Sander-Grinder (Cutting Tool). In addition to sander and grinder attachment both uninstalled and installed tile. The cutting is done dry.

Sandwich Panel. A panel consisting of two outer faces of wood or metal, bonded to a core of insulating foam.

Sash. A frame that holds glass. The framework which holds the glass in a window.

Sash Bead. A strip with one edge molded, against which a sash slides.

Sash, Transom. The framework of a window over a door or window hinged for ventilation, that holds the glass in place.

Saturated Air. Air that contains all of the moisture it an hold. With saturated air, the dry-bulb, wet-bulb, and dew point temperatures are all equal.

Saw Cut. A cut in hardened concrete utilizing diamond or silicone-carbide blades or discs.

Sawed Joints. A joint cut in hardened concrete, generally not to the full depth of the member, by means of special equipment.

Scab. A short piece of lumber used to splice, or to prevent movement of two other pieces.

Scaffolding. A temporary structure for the support of deck forms, cartways, or workmen, or a combination of these such as an elevated platform for supporting workmen, tools, and materials; adjustable metal scaffolding is frequently adapted for shoring in concrete work.

Scantling. Lumber with a cross-section ranging from 2 by 4 inches to 4 by 4 inches.

Scarf Joint. A glued end connection between two pieces of wood, using a sloping cut to create a large surface for the glue bond, to allow it to develop the full tensile strength of the wood it connects.

Scarfing. A joint between two pieces of wood which allows them to be spliced lengthwise.

Scarifier. A piece of thin sheet metal with teeth or serrations cut in the edge. It is used to roughen fresh mortar surfaces to achieve a good bond for the tile. A scarifier also can be used to roughen the surface of concrete.

Scotia. A hollow molding used as a part of a cornice, and often under the nosing of a stair tread.

Scratch Coat. The first coat in a three-coat application of plaster.

Scratcher. Any serrated or sharply tined object that is used to roughen the surface of one coat of mortar to provide a mechanical key for the next coat.

Scratching. The application of a scratch coat and its combing with a scratcher.

Screed. To strike off mortar laying above the desired plane or shape.

Screed. A strip of wood, metal, or plaster that establishes the level to which concrete or plaster will be placed.

Screed Guide. Firmly established grade strips or side forms for unformed concrete which will guide the strikeoff in producing the desired plane or shape.

Scupper. An opening through which water can drain from the edge of a flat roof. An opening cut through a roof system, acting as a waterway so water can be discharged off the roof.

Section. A drawing showing the kind, arrangement, and proportions of the various parts of a structure. It is assumed that the structure is cut by a plane, and the section is the view gained by looking in one direction.

Seiche. A wave on the surface of water in an enclosed or semi-enclosed area (lake, bay or harbor).

Seismic. Relating to earthquakes.

Self-Furring Lath. Metal lath with dimples that space the lath away from the sheathing behind it to allow plaster to penetrate the lath.

Self-Tapping. Creates its own screw threads on the inside of a hole.

Septic Tank. A private sewage system, installed together with a leaching field, that collects sewage and allows the solid waste to settle to the bottom of an area while the liquid particles of the sewage drain into the leaching field area.

Service Disconnect (or, Main Switch). A means of disconnecting an entire building from electrical service.

Set. The condition reached by a cement paste, mortar, or concrete when it has lost plasticity to an arbitrary degree, usually measured in terms of resistance to penetration or deformation; initial set refers to first stiffening; final set refers to attainment of significant rigidity; also, strain remaining after removal of stress.

Setting Bed. The layer of mortar on which the tile is set. The final coat of mortar on a wall or ceiling also may be called a setting bed.

Shaft. An unbroken vertical passage through a multistory building, used for elevators, wiring, plumbing, ductwork, etc.

Shear Connector. Steel stud or strap, embedded within concrete slab, to transfer horizontal shear loads from slab to supporting structure.

Shear Panel. A vertical plane (wall) that resists lateral forces.

Shear Strength. The strength of an element to resist shear.

Shearwall. A wall designed to resist forces. A wall portion of a structural frame intended to resist lateral forces, such as earthquake, wind, and blast, acting in or parallel to the plane of the wall.

Sheathing. The rough covering applied to the outside of the roof, wall, or floor framing of a structure. Wall boards, roofing boards; generally applied to narrow boards laid with a space between them, according to the length of a shingle exposed to weather.

Shed. A building or dormer with a single pitched roof.

Sheet Flashing. A thin piece of treated metal placed in construction to direct the flow of water or to prevent water penetration.

Sheet Piling. Planking or sheeting made of concrete, timber, metal or steel that is driven in, interlocked or are tongue and grooved in close contact to provide a tight wall to resist the lateral pressure of water, adjacent earth or other materials.

Sheetrock. Plasterboard sheets.

Shell (Concrete). Concrete outside the transverse reinforcement confining the concrete.

Shell (Masonry). The outer portion of a hollow masonry unit as placed in masonry.

Shim. A thin piece of material placed between two components of a building to adjust their relative positions as they are assembled; to insert shims.

Shop Drawings. Drawings of specific items of the project provided by subcontractors.

Shop Painted. Coating(s) of paint applied in shop, usually a primer coat to protect metal from corrosion, which may or may not receive additional coats in the field.

Short-Circuiting. Situation that occurs when the supply air flows to exhaust registers before entering the breathing zone. To avoid short-circuiting, the supply air must be delivered at a temperature and velocity the results in mixing throughout the space.

Shotcrete. A low-slump concrete mixture deposited by being blown from a nozzle at high speed with a stream of compressed air.

Shower Pan. Terminology used in some areas for Waterproof membrane.

Shrinkage. The decrease in volume, or contraction, of a material by the escape of any volatile substance, or by a chemical or physical change in the material.

Shrinkage Cracking. Cracking of a structure or member due to failure in tension caused by external or internal restraints as reduction in moisture content develops, or as carbonation occurs, or both.

Sidelight. A tall, narrow window alongside a door.

Siding. The outside finish between the casings.

Sills. The horizontal timbers of a house which either rest upon the masonry foundations or, in the absence of such, form the foundation.

Simple Beam. A beam that is supported on two supports and where no bending is transferred from the beam to the support.

Single-Hung Window. A window with two overlapping sashes, the lower of which can slide vertically in tracks, and the upper of which is fixed.

Sister Joist. The reinforcement of a joist by nailing or attaching a stronger piece to a weaker one.

Sizing. Working material to the desired size; a coating of glue, shellac, or other substance applied to a surface to prepare it for painting or other method of finish.

Sleeper. A timber laid on the ground to support a floor joist.

Slenderness Ratio. The ratio of the unbraced length of the column to the least dimension.

Slip Coating. A ceramic material or mixture other than a glaze, applied to a ceramic body and fired to the maturity required to develop specified characteristics.

Slip Forming. Building multistory sitecast concrete walls with forms that rise up the wall as construction progresses.

Slot, Anchor. A groove in an object into which a fastener or connector is inserted to attach objects together.

Slot Cut. Description of a tile that has been cut to fit around pipes or switch boxes. This tile is usually in the shape of the letter H or the letter L.

Slump. A measure of consistency of freshly mixed concrete, mortar, or stucco equal to the subsidence measured.

Slump Cone. A mold in the form of the lateral surface of the frustum of a cone with a base diameter of 8 in. (203 mm), top diameter 4 in. (102 mm), and height 12 in. (305 mm), used for fabricate a specimen of freshly mixed concrete for the slump test; a cone 6 in. (152 mm) high is used for tests of freshly mixed mortar and stucco.

Slurry. A mixture of water and any finely divided insoluble material, such as portland cement, slag, or clay in suspension.

Sodium Light. An electric lamp that contains sodium vapor and electrodes between which a luminous discharge takes place and that is used for lighting highways.

Soffit. The underside of a part of member of a structure, such as a beam, stairway, or arch. The undersurface of a horizontal element of a building, especially the underside of a stair or a roof overhang.

Softwood Plywood Panel. Plywood manufactured from softwood species (coniferous trees with needlelike or scalelike (eaves) species such as Douglas fir, western larch, western hemlock Sitka spruce, white cedars, or redwood.

Soil and Waste Pipe. Either plastic, copper, cast iron or DWV drainage, water and vent.

Soil Gases. Gases that enter a building from the surrounding ground (e.g., radon, volatile organics, pesticides).

Soil Stack. A vertical pipe used to carry human waste from toilets.

Soldier. A brick laid on its end, with its narrow face toward the outside of the wall.

Sole Plate. The horizontal piece of dimension lumber at the bottom of the studs in a wall in a light frame building.

Sound Absorption Coefficient. The ratio of sound energy absorbed to the sound energy hitting a surface.

Sound Attenuation. A process in which sound is reduced as its energy is converted to motion or heat.

Sound Transmission Loss (STL). The decrease or attenuation in sound energy, in decibels, of airborne sound as it passes through a building material. In general, transmission loss increases with frequency, the higher the frequency, the greater the sound transmission loss.

Space Frame, Space Truss. A truss that spans with two-way action.

Spall. A fragment, usually in the shape of a flake, detached from a larger mass by a blow, by the action of weather, by pressure, or by expansion within the larger mass.

Span. The distance between supports for a beam, girder, truss, vault, arch or other horizontal structural device; to carry a load between supports. The distance between the bearings of a timber or arch.

Spandrel. That part of a wall between the head of a window and the sill of the window above it.

Specific Gravity. The ratio of the weight of any volume of a mass or substance to the weight of an equal volume of water at a given temperature. The specific gravity of a substance times the density of water equals the density of the substance.

Spiral Reinforcing. Continuously wound reinforcing in the form of a cylindrical helix.

Splash Block. A small precast block of concrete or plastic used to divert water at the bottom of a downspout.

Split Jamb. A door frame fabricated in two interlocking halves, to be installed from the opposite sides of an opening.

Split Ring. A connector for timbers consisting of a metal ring set in circular grooves in two pieces. The assembly is held together by bolts.

Spool Insulator. A device designed and used to support a conductor and electrically separate it from other conductors or objects.

Square. A tool used by mechanics to obtain accuracy; a term applied to a surface including 100 square feet.

Stability. The ability to remain unchanged; equilibrium, steady, constant. Ability to restore to original condition after being disturbed by some force.

Stability. Refers to the quality of being stable, or having the capability of remaining in position.

Stack Effect. Pressure-driven airflow produced by convection as heated air rises, creating a positive pressure area at the top of a building and a negative pressure area at the bottom of a building. The tack effect can overpower the mechanical system and disrupt ventilation and circulation in a building.

Stack Vent. A vent (pipe) that connects to a soil or waster stack above the highest fixture in the system.

Staging. Temporary scaffolding with platforms placed in and around a building to create working spaces.

Stainless Reglet. A groove in a wall to receive flashing which is constructed of an alloy of steel and has resistance to corrosion.

Stair Pan. A stair assembly constructed to hold precast or cast-in place masonry or stone in metal sheet pans at the treads.

Stair Tread, Metal-Pan Concrete Filled. Section formed from sheet metal to receive concrete fill which will function as stair tread.

Standing Seam. A sheet metal roofing seam that projects at right angles to the plane of the roof.

Standing-Seam Roof. A sheet metal roof system that has a roofing seam that projects at right angles to the plane of the roof.

Standpipe. A pipe that extends the full height of a building, used to provide water exclusively for the fighting of fires. A dry standpipe does not have water directly connected to it. A wet standpipe is directly connected to a water supply. This pipe is usually located in a stairway.

Staple. Double pointed, U-shaped piece of metal used for same purposes as nails, but providing additional head holding power.

Starter. A device that insures that a motor does not receive too high a current when starting up.

Static. State of being at rest, having no motion.

Steam Curing. Curing of concrete or mortar in water vapor at atmospheric or higher pressures and at temperatures between about 100 and 420 F (40 and 215 C).

Steel Structural. Steel that is rolled in a variety of shapes and manufactured for use as structural load-bearing members.

Steel Tread. The horizontal part of a stair system, manufactured from steel.

Stiffener Plate. A steel plate attached to a structural member to support it against heavy localized loadings or stresses.

Stiffness. The quality of resistance to deformation on the part of a material, a component member of a structure, or the whole structure.

Stile. A vertical framing member in a panel door.

Still Water. A part of a stream where the gradient is so gentle that no current is visible.

Stirrup. A vertical loop of steel bar used to reinforce a concrete beam against diagonal tension forces.

Stirrup-Tie. A stirrup that forms a complete loop, as differentiated from a U-stirrup, which has an open top.

Storm Window. A sash added to the outside of a window in winter to increase its thermal resistance and decrease air infiltration.

Straightedge. A straight piece of lumber that is used to rod mortar and to align tile.

Strain. Change in shape of a material due to stress.

Strap Channel. A U-shaped or L-shaped iron plate for connecting two or more timbers.

Strength Design. A design theory used for most reinforced concrete designs. A design in which members are designed to fail. Safety is not provided by limiting stresses, but by using a factored load that is greater than the actual load.

Strength Reduction Factor. A factor introduced into the calculation of strength design in reinforced concrete, which increases actual loading, providing an added factor of safety.

Stress. The internal force of a body that resists external force.

Stretcher. A brick or masonry unit laid in its most usual position, with the broadest surface of the unit horizontal and the length of the unit parallel to the surface of the wall.

Striking Joints. A process of removing excess grout from the joints by wiping with a sponge or cloth or scraping with a curved instrument.

Stringer. The sloping wood or steel member supporting the treads of a stair. A long horizontal timber in a structure supporting a floor.

Structural - Use Panel Diaphragm. Structural-use panel sheathing on floors, roofs, or walls which provides shear strength to resist wind and earthquake loads.

Structural Bond. The interlocking pattern of masonry units used to tie two or more wythes together in a wall.

Structural Diaphragms. Structural members, such as floor and roof slabs, which transmit internal forces to lateral-force-resisting members.

Structure. That which gives form to something and works to resist changes in the form due to the action of various forces.

Structure Borne Sound. A condition in which the sound waves are carried by a solid material.

Strut. A compression member, a column, usually implying that it can be placed at any angle, not just vertically.

Stucco. A cement plaster used for coating exterior walls and other exterior surfaces of buildings. Portland cement plaster used as an exterior cladding or siding material. A fine plaster used for interior decoration and fine work.

Stud. Vertical member of appropriate size (2x4 to 4x10 in.) (50x100 to 100x250 mm) and spacing 16in to 30 in.) (400 to 750 mm) to support sheathing of concrete forms; also a headed steel device used to anchor steel plates or shapes to concrete members. One of a set of small vertical elements, usually wood, used to produce a frame wall. An upright beam in the framework of a building.

Studding. The framework of a partition or the wall of a house; usually referred to as 2 by 4's.

Sub-Flooring. Certain materials like plywood, that is mounted to the floor joints of a building or structure, onto which the walls and finished floor is attached.

Subdiaphragm. A portion of a larger wood diaphragm designed to anchor and transfer local forces to primary diaphragm struts and the main diaphragm.

Subduction. The sinking of a plate under an overriding plate in a convergence zone.

Subfloor. A wood floor which is laid over the floor joists and on which the finished floor is laid.

Subpurlin. A very small roof framing member that spans between joists and purlins.

Substrate. The underlying support for the ceramic tile installation.

Surveying. A branch of applied mathematics, including geometry and trigonometry, that aids in determining and delineating the form, extent and position of land.

Suspended Ceiling. A finish ceiling that is hung on wires from the structure above.

Suspended Structure. A structure supported principally by tension members or carrying its loads principally in tension.

Swale Excavation. The digging up of low-lying land such as a small meadow, swamp, or marshy depression.

Switchgear (Switchboard). A freestanding assembly including primary (disconnect) switches, secondary (feeder) switches, and overcurrent protection device (fuses and circuit breakers).

T&G Siding. Tongue and groove exterior siding.

Tack Coat. Application of material made from asphalt on old surface to insure its bond to new construction.

Take-Off Man. Someone who can read blueprints and is familiar with the specifications. This person makes details concerning the project after gathering the necessary information and then the estimator estimates the labor, material quantities, and special items needed to complete the job.

Tapping Valve. A device to open or close a duct, pipe, or other passage, or to regulate flow which has been pierced by another device for tapping into the flow.

Tarpaulin. A waterproofed canvas or other material used for protecting athletic fields, goods or other exposed objects or areas.

Tee. A metal or precast concrete member with a cross section resembling the letter "T".

Tendon. A steel strand used for prestressing a concrete member.

Tensile Strength. The pulling force necessary to break a given specimen divided by the cross sectional area. Units given in lbs./in.2 (P.S.I.). It measures the resistance of a material to stretching without rupture. Normally is not used with reference to elastic materials which recover after elongation.

Tension. Stress which tends to elongate a member.

Tension Ring. A structural element, forming a closed curve in plan, which is in tension because of the action of the test of the structure.

Terminal Adapters. Electrical fittings attached to the end of a conductor or to a piece of equipment for taking power from an outlet in a way for which it was not designed.

Terminal Box. A box, usually with a removable cover, that contains leads from electrical equipment ready for connection to a power source.

Terne. An allow of lead and tin, used to coat sheets of carbon steel or stainless steel for use as metal roofing sheet.

Terra Cotta. Hard baked clayware, including tile, of variable color, averaging reddish red-yellow in hue and of high saturation.

Terrazzo. A finish floor material consisting of concrete with an aggregate of marble chips selected for size and color, which is ground and polished smooth after curing.

Test Pile. To measure the deviation of a pile in the horizontal and vertical planes.

Thermal Conductivity. Ability of a material to conduct heat; physical constant for quantity of heat that passes through unit volume of a substance in unit of time when difference in temperature of two opposite faces is one degree.

Thermal Lag Factor. The time interval between the time heat enters a material at one side and exits at the other side.

Thermodynamics. The science dealing with the relationship between heat and other forms of energy.

Thermoplastic. Having the property of softening when heated and rehardening when cooled.

Thermostat. An automatic device for regulating the supply of gas or electricity to a heating apparatus. A device for actuating fire alarms or for controlling automatic sprinklers.

Thin-set. A term used to describe the bonding of tile with suitable materials applied approximately 1/8" thick.

Threshold. The beveled piece over which the door swings; sometimes called a carpet strip.

Thrust. A lateral or inclined force resulting from the structural action of an arch, vault, dome, suspension structure, or rigid frame.

Tie. A device for holding two part of a construction together, a structural device that acts in tension.

Tie Beam. A reinforced concrete beam cast as part of a masonry wall, whose primary purpose is to hold the wall together, especially against seismic loads, or cast between a number of isolated foundation elements to maintain their relative positions.

Tie Rod. A steel rod that acts in tension.

Tie Strap. A metal plate that fastens two parts together as a post, rod or beam.

Tie Wire. The 18-gauge galvanized wire used in construction work.

Tied Column. A square or rectangular reinforced concrete column containing longitudinal reinforcing and lateral ties.

Tile. A fired clay product that is thin in cross section as compared to a brick, either a thin, flat element (ceramic tile or quarry tile), a thin, curved element (roofing tile), or a hollow element with thin walls.

Timber. Lumber with cross-section over 4 by 6 inches, such as posts, sills, and girders.

To the Weather. A term applied to the projecting of shingles or siding beyond the course above.

Toe Plate. A metal bar fastened to the outer edge of a grating, rear of a tread, or bottom rail of a door.

Tongue and Groove. A type of lumber or precast concrete pile having mated projecting and grooved edges to provide a tight fit, abbreviated "T & G".

Top Plate. The horizontal member at the top of a stud wall. Piece of lumber supporting ends of rafters.

Topping, Concrete. Concrete layer placed to form a floor surface on a concrete base.

Torque. Twisting action; moment.

Torsion. The rotation of a diaphragm caused by lateral forces and whose center of mass does not coincide with the center of rigidity.

Tower Cooling. A device usually placed on a roof for cooling water used in air conditioning. A structure through which heated water is circulated.

Trammel Bar. A trammel bar, which is easy to construct, is more accurate than many other layout tools. It is used to erect perpendicular lines and to bisect angles. The tile setter can make a trammel bar from a stick of a size that is suitable for the particular job.

Transfer. That act of transferring stress in prestressing tendons from jacks or pretensioning bed to concrete member.

Transformer. A device that changes, or transforms, alternating current from one voltage to another.

Transit-Mixed Concrete. Concrete mixed in a drum on the back of a truck as it is transported to the building code.

Translate. To move from one place to another, without rotation. Motion of a body along a line without rotation or turning.

Transom. A transverse piece in a structure, lintel. A horizontal crossbar in a window, over a door, or between a door and a window or a fanlight above it. A window above a door or other window built on and commonly hinged to a transom.

Transverse. Across, at right angles to the main axis of a structural member.

Trap. Located at a plumbing fixture, designed to hold a quantity of water that prevents gasses in the sewer system from entering a room.

Tread. One of the horizontal planes of a stair or step.

Tremie. A large funnel with a tube attached, used to deliver concrete into deep forms or beneath water or slurry.

Trench. A long and narrow deep trough in the sea floor; interpreted as marking the line along which a plate bends down into a subduction zone.

Trim. A term sometimes applied to outside or interior finished woodwork and the finish around openings.

Trimmer. The beam or floor joist into which a header is framed.

Troffer. A channel-like enclosure for light sources.

Trowel Finish. The final finish of concrete, plaster, stucco, etc., by the use of a hand trowel.

Truss. A triangular arrangement of structural members that reduces nonaxial forces on the truss to a set of axial forces in the members. Structural framework of triangular units for supporting loads over long spans.

Tsunami. A sea wave produced by a large displacement of the ocean bottom, the result of earthquakes or volcanic activity.

TWA. Time-weighted Average. In air sampling, this refers to the average air concentration of contaminants during a particular sampling period.

Two-Way Action. Bending of a slab or deck in which bending stresses are approximately equal in the two principal directions of the structure.

Two-Way Concrete Joist System. A reinforced concrete framing system in which columns directly support an orthogonal grid of intersecting joists.

U Bolt. A U-shaped, bent iron bar that has bolts and threads at both ends.

UL. Underwriters Laboratories, Inc., 333 Pfingsten Road, Northbrook, Illinois 60062, (708) 272-8800.

Unbonded Construction. Post-tensioned concrete construction in which the tendons are not grouted to the surrounding concrete.

Undercourse. A course of shingles laid beneath an exposed course of shingles at the lower edge of a wall or roof, in order to provide a waterproof layer behind the joints in the exposed course.

Underdrain. Perforated pipe drain installed in a wedge of stone under a slab to intercept ground water and drain it off.

Underlayment. A layer of hardboard, particleboard, plywood, mastic with latex binders, mastic with asphalt binders, mastic with polyvinyl-acetate, etc., placed to cover subfloor irregularities, to absorb the movement of wood subfloors and to provide a smooth surface for the finish material.

Union Brass. A pipe fitting constructed of brass, used to join two pipes without turning either pipe.

Union Hub. A pipe fitting used to join two pipes without turning either pipe, with one end of the fitting enlarged into a bell or socket.

Unit Substation. A freestanding assembly including a transformer, switchgear and meter(s).

Unit-and-Mullion System. A curtain wall system consisting of prefabricated panel units secured with site-applied mullions.

Upside-Down Roof. A membrane roof assembly in which the thermal insulation lies above the membrane.

Utility Pole. A vertical pole with cross arms, where power company service drops its wires to a service switch on a building or structure.

Valley. A trough formed by the intersection of two roof slopes.

Valley Rafter. A diagonal rafter that supports a roof valley.

Vapor Barrier. Waterproof membrane placed under concrete floor slabs that are placed on grade.

Vapor Retarder. A layer of material intended to obstruct the passage of water vapor through a building assembly. Also called, less accurately, vapor barrier. Sealing material place between building components or materials to arrest movement of moisture within building enclosure assembly.

Vault. An arched surface. An arch translated along an axis normal to the plane of its centerline curve.

Veneer, Ashlar. An ornamental or protective facing of masonry composed of squared stones.

Vent, Foundation. Opening in foundation wall to provide natural ventilation to foundation crawl spaces.

Vent Soffit. An opening under the eaves of a roof used to allow air to flow into the attic or the space below the roof sheathing.

Vestibule. An entrance to a house; usually enclosed.

Vinyl Sheet. The rolled form of vinyl.

Vision Panel. Glass placed in an opening of a door.

Vitreous. That degree of vitrification evidence by low water absorption. Note: The term vitreous generally signifies less than 0.5% absorption for fixtures, except for floor and wall tile and low-voltage electrical porcelain which are considered vitreous up to 3.0% water absorption.

Vitreous Tile. Tile with water absorption of more than 0.5%, but not more than 3.0%.

Vitrification. The progressive reduction in porosity of a ceramic composition as a result of heat treatment, or the process involved.

Vitrified Clay Pipe. Pipes used especially for underground drainage, that are made of clay baked hard and then glazed so they are impervious to water.

Void. An unfilled space in a material of trapped air or other gas.

Volt. Electricity is caused by creating a higher pressure electric charge at one point in a conductor than at another. This potential difference is called voltage, or volt.

Waferboard. A building panel made by bonding together large, flat flakes of wood.

Waffle Slab. A two-way concrete joist system. Two-way slab or flat slab made up of a double system of narrow ribs or joists, usually at right angles to each other, forming a pattern of waffle-like coffers.

Wainscoting. A wall facing, usually of wood, cut stone, or ceramic tile, that is carried only part way up a wall. Matched boarding or panel work covering the lower portion of a wall.

Wale. A horizontal beam.

Wall. A member, usually vertical, used to enclose or separate spaces.

Wall Tie. A mechanical metal fastener which connects wythes of masonry to each other or to other materials.

Waste Stack. A vertical pipe that carries liquids other than human waste.

Water Absorption. The ability to take up and retain water.

Water Cooled Condenser. A condenser in which water is normally circulated through a cooling tower through which heat is distributed to the atmosphere.

Water Hammer. Noise, in a water pipe, occurring when air is trapped in the pipe and collides with the pipe wall at a change in the direction of the pipe.

Water Table. The level at which the pressure of water in the soil is equal to atmospheric pressure; effectively, the level to which ground water will fill an excavation. The finish at the bottom of a house which carries water away from the foundation.

Water Table Molding. A projection on the bottom of an exterior wall to prevent rain or water from seeping through to the wall below.

Water Vapor. Water in its gaseous phase.

Waterproofing. The act or process of making something waterproof. A coating capable of imparting waterproofness.

Waterstop. A synthetic rubber strip used to seal joints in concrete foundation walls.

Wearing Course. A topping or surface treatment to increase the resistance of a concrete pavement or slab to abrasion.

Weather Seal. A flanged channel installed on the top of an exterior door.

Weathered Joint. A mortar joint finished in a sloping, planar profile that tends to shed water to the outside of the wall.

Weatherstrip. A ribbon of resilient material used to reduce air infiltration through the crack around a sash or door.

Web. In a roller or built-up steel beam, the vertical plate connecting the top and bottom flanges.

Web (Masonry). An interior solid portion of a hollow-masonry unit as placed in masonry.

Weep Hole. A small opening, the purpose of which is to permit drainage of water that accumulates inside a building component.

Well. A pit or hole sunk into the earth to reach a supply of water. An open space extending vertically through floors of a structure.

Wellpoint. A perforated pipe surrounded by sand to permit the pumping of ground water.

Wellpoint System. A series of vertical pipes in the ground connected to a header and pump to drain marshy areas or to control ground seepage.

Wheel Barrow. A small vehicle with handles and one or more wheels used for carrying small loads.

Wind ("i" Pronounced as in "Kind"). A term used to describe the surface of a board when twisted (winding) or when resting upon two diagonally opposite corners, if laid upon a perfectly flat surface.

Wind Drift. Horizontal deflection of a frame caused by wind forces.

Wind Load. A load on a building caused by wind pressure.

Wind Uplift. Upward forces on a structure caused by negative aerodynamic pressures that result from certain wind conditions.

Winder. A stair tread that is wider at one end than at the other.

Window Well. Recess created in grade outside window located at or below grade to allow for natural light to reach window, often created by use of corrugated metal in half-round shape.

Wireway. A sheet metal trough with hinge or removable cover to carry up to 30 cables.

Wobble Friction. In prestressed concrete, is friction caused by unintended deviation of prestressing sheath or duct from its specified profile.

Wood Base. Wood strip applied to base of wall to protect wall surface and finish intersection of wall and floor.

Wood Fascia. Flat wood member of cornice or other finish, generally board of cornice to which gutter is secured.

Wood Float. The wood float is sometimes used in place of the flat trowel for floating mortar. It is good for smoothing small irregularities left on the mortar bed, working the surface of the mortar before troweling on the pure coat, or compacting floor and deck mortar.

Wood Frame. Floors, roofs, exterior and bearing walls of a building or structure constructed only with wood.

Wood Nailer. Strip of wood attached to steel or concrete to facilitate making nailed connections.

Wood Riser. The vertical wood board under the tread in a stairway system.

Wood Roof Nailer. Wood strip (usually in plane of roof insulation) secured to structural roof deck used for securing roofing membrane.

Wood Structural Panel. A structural panel product composed primarily of wood. Wood structural panels include all-veneer plywood, composite panels containing a combination of veneer and wood-based material, and mat-formed panels such as oriented strand board and waferboard.

Workability. The property of freshly mixed concrete or mortar which determines the ease and homogeneity with which it can be mixed, placed, compacted, and finished.

Working drawings. Drawings of the project used during construction.

Working Stress. The maximum permissible stress used in the design of a member.

Working Stress Design. A design theory that is used in the design of concrete and masonry members. Safety is provided by limiting allowable stresses.

Wye. A pipe fitting which joins three pipes at a 45 degree angle.

Wythe. A vertical layer of masonry one masonry unit thick. (Rhymes with "scythe" and "tithe".)

Yield Point. The point at which a material deforms with no increase in load. The stress at which a material ceases to deform in a fully elastic manner.

Yield Strength. The stress at which a material ceases to deform in a fully elastic manner.

Z-Tie Wall. A Z-shaped bar used as a support bracket.

Zero-Slump Concrete. A concrete mixed with so little water that it has a slump of zero.

A

B

C

D

E

F

G

I

J

L

M

N

O

P

R

S

T

U

V

W